OPERATION SIDEWINDER

OPERATION

SIDEWINDER

a play in two acts by
SAM SHEPARD

THE BOBBS-MERRILL CO., INC.

Indianapolis • New York

The Bobbs-Merrill Company, Inc.
A Subsidiary of Howard W. Sams & Co., Inc.
Publishers/Indianapolis and New York

Library of Congress Catalogue Card Number: 74-108166
Designed by Inese Burunovsky
Manufactured in the United States of America

DEDICATED TO THE FOLLOWING
FOR THEIR KEEN INSPIRATION:

MICHELANGELO ANTONIONI
DAPPER TOMMY THOMPSON
CRAZY HORSE
THE STONES
THE HOLY MODAL ROUNDERS
THE HOPI
NANCY
GABBY HAYES
OLD ORAIBI
MICKEY FREE
1968
O-LAN

OPERATION SIDEWINDER was first produced on March 12, 1970, at the Repertory Theater of Lincoln Center/Vivian Beaumont Theater, New York City, with the following cast in order of appearance:

DUKIE	Robert Phalen
HONEY	Barbara eda-Young
MECHANIC	Michael Miller
YOUNG MAN	Andy Robinson
FOREST RANGER	Robert Riggs
BILLY	Roberts Blossom
COLONEL WARNER	Joseph Mascolo
CAPTAIN	Robert Phalen
CADET	Gus Fleming
MICKEY FREE	Don Plumley
1st COHORT TO MICKEY FREE	Ralph Drischell
2nd COHORT TO MICKEY FREE	Arthur Sellers
CARHOP	Catherine Burns
BLOOD	Garrett Morris
BLADE	Paul Benjamin
DUDE	Charles Pegues
GENERAL BROWSER	Paul Sparer
DOCTOR VECTOR	Ray Fry
SPIDER LADY	Michael Levin
EDITH	Joan Pringle
CAPTAIN BOVINE	Philip Bosco
INDIANS	José Barrera, Paul Benjamin, Gregory Borst, Gus Fleming, Robert Keesler, Michael Levin, Clark Luis, Richard Mason, Muriel Miguel, Louis Mofsie, Santos Morales, Garrett Morris, Jean-Daniel Noland, Joan Pringle, Barbara Spiegel

1st DESERT TACTICAL TROOP ...... Robert Priggs
2nd DESERT TACTICAL TROOP .... Robert Phalen
3rd DESERT TACTICAL TROOP .... Michael Miller

Directed by Michael A. Schultz
Settings designed by Douglas W. Schmidt
Lighting designed by John Gleason

ACT ONE
OPERATION

SIDEWINDER

JESSE JAMES

SCENE 1

The houselights come down. The stage is black. The sound of a rattlesnake rattling. A coyote in the distance. The rattle grows louder. A soft blue light fills the ceiling of the stage then flashes off. A bright flash of yellow light from the center of the stage floor then black again. The blue light comes on and goes out. Again the yellow light flashes, then comes on again slowly and glows brightly, with the rest of the stage dark. It forms almost a perfect circle. In the center of the circle can be seen a very large sidewinder rattlesnake, coiled and ready to strike. The light seems to be coming from the snake itself. When stretched to its full length the sidewinder measures over six feet and looks like it weighs over thirty pounds. The eyes are ruby red and blink on and off. The tongue spits. The rattle rattles. The snake's skin is bright yellow with black diamonds. It undulates in a mechanical rhythm. Its hissing grows louder and the rattle too. The head sways from side to side. Sound of a jet going across the sky very loudly, then into silence, then a sonic boom. Silence. Sound of a car passing on a highway. A MAN'S VOICE is heard.

MAN'S VOICE
Look, Honey!

Sound of car screeching to stop, then backing up, then stopping again. Sound of car door slamming. Bright yellow desert light comes up and fills the stage, making it hard to see the snake except for the black diamonds and the ruby eyes. The snake keeps up its rhythmic rattle, sway, blink, hiss as the MAN enters from stage left with a fancy looking movie camera, straw cowboy hat, open shirt, hairy chest, Bermuda shorts and Hush Puppies. He yells back off left.

3

MAN

Bring the tripod, Honey! Hurry up!

He starts focusing his camera on the sidewinder and inching in on it, taking his eye away from the view finder every once in a while to make sure he's not getting too close. HONEY, a very sexy chick with long blonde hair and tight pants, high heels, etc., comes running on from left with a tripod.

Take it easy! Not so fast! We don't want to get him aggravated.

HONEY

Boy, what a monster! I've never see one so huge.

She hands him the tripod. The MAN sets up the camera on the tripod and moves in for a close shot.

Be careful, Dukie. They're deadly poisonous. I read it in one of those desert manuals. They're the only thing to really be afraid of out here.

MAN

Don't worry. I didn't spend the best part of my years in the Philippines for nothing you know.

HONEY makes a wide circle around the sidewinder as she talks and the sound of the camera whirring is heard as the MAN shoots. The sidewinder just keeps up his tense rhythm.

HONEY

He's actually kind of beautiful when you look at him close. I was always taught to be afraid of snakes but actually they're not so bad. I mean he's just out here trying to get a suntan or something. There's nothing awful about that. He looks kind of tense but I'll bet he'd loosen up in no time at all if he got the right kind of attention. You know what I mean, Dukie? Little mice and stuff. I'll bet he'd make a nice pet.

The MAN straightens up from his camera.

MAN

Maybe we oughta' aggravate him a little, Honey. He blends right into the background when he's not moving. I don't want to waste any more film than I have to.

HONEY

O.K.

She stomps her foot and hisses at the sidewinder.

MAN

Now wait a minute! For crying out loud! Not like that.

HONEY

Well how then?

MAN

Well I don't know. Aren't there some stones around we could throw at him?

HONEY

Nope. Just sand.

MAN

Well how about a stick then?

HONEY

I don't see any.

Suddenly the sidewinder leaps out and grabs HONEY around the neck and pulls her to the ground. She screams. The MAN jumps and crashes into his camera; it smashes to pieces. He falls on the ground and frantically scrambles away as the snake coils around HONEY's body. She screams and kicks but the sidewinder coils tighter so that it's completely wrapped around her from her neck to her feet. The MAN watches on his hands and knees as the eyes of the sidewinder blink, the tongue spits and hisses, and the rattle rattles.

MAN

Now, Honey, take it easy! Don't fight it. You'll just make him madder than he already is. Just relax and I'll go try to find a Forest Ranger.

HONEY

Oh fuck! He's really got me. Don't leave! Dukie!

MAN

I'll be right back. Try to relax, Honey. Don't make a move until I get back.

He runs off right.

BLACKOUT

The song "Do It Girl" comes on in the blackout. The red eyes of the sidewinder blink in the dark.

OPERATION SIDEWINDER
music by HOLY MODAL ROUNDERS

DO IT GIRL

Everytime I see you wanna do it girl
Right out in the street I wanna do it girl
In front of everybody wanna do it girl
I'm losing my control I feel it in my soul

I wanna do it I wanna do it
I wanna do it, do it, do it, do it,
do it, do it, do it, do it, do it

Like a reindeer in the tundra
Wanna do it girl
Like a reptile on a mesa
Wanna do it girl
Like a tiger in the jungle
Wanna do it girl
So lay it on the line
I need you all the time

I wanna do it I wanna do it
I wanna do it, do it, do it, do it,
do it, do it, do it, do it, do it

I know you're going to love the
Way I do it girl
I know you're going to bless the day
I do it girl
There really isn't much to say
But do it girl
The time is going fast, so let the
Good times last

I wanna do it I wanna do it
I wanna do it, do it, do it, do it,
do it, do it, do it, do it, do it

by PETER STAMPFEL & ANTONIA

SCENE

The song fades out. The blinking red eyes turn to yellow lights and slowly rise about ten feet off the ground.

Voices are heard in the dark as the lights fade up and reveal a small Volkswagen in the air on a hydraulic lift with the tail end facing the audience, its yellow tail lights blinking on and off. Below the car is a MECHANIC dressed in greasy coveralls holding a wrench, rag and oil can. Next to him is a YOUNG MAN with long blond hair down to his shoulders, a bright purple T shirt, tight leather pants and bare feet. They are both looking up underneath the car with their backs turned toward the audience as they talk.

MECHANIC

So for no reason at all they just all of a sudden started blinkin' on and off?

YOUNG MAN

Well it seemed like the whole car shook for a second and then they started to blink. All the lights.

MECHANIC

Well, it could be your voltage regulator or the generator. I'll just check out yer wiring here to make sure.

YOUNG MAN
Thanks.

MECHANIC

Could've picked yerself a better time to make a

movie ya' know. Days get pretty hot and long this
time a' year.

YOUNG MAN
        Yeah. I know.

MECHANIC
        Even the all year arounders usually leave 'round
        about now. They migrate around May or June at
        the latest, then come back toward the tail end of
        September.

YOUNG MAN
        Where do they go?

MECHANIC
        Oh, some move into the San Berdoo Valley, some
        even go to Hollywood, L.A., around in there.

YOUNG MAN
        No kidding.

MECHANIC
        Yeah. You come here from there and they go there
        from here. Crazy.

YOUNG MAN
        Crazy.

MECHANIC
        I suppose what with all the earthquake scares and
        riots and all there's gonna be a lot more folks movin'
        out here in the desert.

YOUNG MAN
Yeah. I suppose.

The MECHANIC fiddles around with some wires under the car. The YOUNG MAN is getting impatient.

MECHANIC
Well, you're gettin' paid good for your work so why should you care. How much do you get for a movie anyway?

YOUNG MAN
It depends.

MECHANIC
At least a thousand, right?

YOUNG MAN
At least.

MECHANIC
Where'd you go to College?

YOUNG MAN
I didn't.

MECHANIC
Me neither. I'm in the wrong racket though. You know how many months I gotta work to clear a thousand? Take a guess.

YOUNG MAN
A million months. Look, what about my car? Can I get going pretty soon?

MECHANIC

Sure, sure. . . .

*A pistol falls from under the car onto the ground. The ME-
CHANIC looks at it then at the YOUNG MAN. The YOUNG
MAN bends down and picks it up.*

Say, you better hadn't let the Ranger catch you with
that thing, son. No firearms allowed in the National
Monument.

YOUNG MAN

Oh, it's all right. It's not mine. I'm taking it to a
friend of mine who lives on the desert. It's his. I had
it cleaned for him and put a new chamber in. He's a
prospector so he never gets a chance to come into
town much. So I told him I'd do it for him.

MECHANIC

Well I never heard of no prospector using a weapon
like that.

*Sound of a car coming up fast and screeching to a stop.
The YOUNG MAN tries to hide the gun in his pants but it
won't fit so he just sticks his hand inside his shirt with the
pistol bulging out. The MAN from the first scene rushes on
from stage right.*

MAN

Oh——oh——help——I need some help. Anyone.
You've got to come quick. Help——

MECHANIC

Take her easy there, mister. Catch your breath. I'll
get you something to set on.

The MECHANIC goes off right and comes back with a wooden crate. The MAN is panting and looking at the YOUNG MAN who is getting up tight. The MECHANIC sets down the crate and sits the MAN down.

Here now. Here. Sit down for a second and get your breath back.

MAN

Oh——you've got to send help.

MECHANIC

What's the problem now?

MAN

My wife. Honey. My wife. She——

YOUNG MAN

What about my car!

MECHANIC

What *about* your wife?

MAN

She's——she's been attacked.

MECHANIC

Attacked?

YOUNG MAN

Come off it.

MAN
> By a snake.

MECHANIC
> You mean she got bit? Was it a rattler?

MAN
> A huge snake.

MECHANIC
> Now calm down and try to tell me where she was
> bit. It's important.

MAN
> In the neck. Then——all over. All over.

*The YOUNG MAN whips out the pistol and holds it on the
MECHANIC.*

YOUNG MAN
> Now stop fucking around and fix my car, you dumb
> grease monkey!

MECHANIC
> Now just a second, kid.

MAN
> You've got to help me. My wife's going to die!

*The MAN becomes hysterical and jumps up from the crate,
rushing toward the YOUNG MAN who fires the pistol hitting the MAN in the stomach and sending him backwards.
He lies in a heap, dead. The MECHANIC moves toward
him. The YOUNG MAN stops him with the gun.*

YOUNG MAN

Hold it! Get my car down off the rack! Hurry up!
Get it down!

MECHANIC

You're in some pickle now, son.

YOUNG MAN

Don't say anything. Just get my car down!

MECHANIC

And what if I don't?

YOUNG MAN

Then *I'll* get it down!

*He fires again, hitting the MECHANIC in the stomach. The
MECHANIC falls back on top of the MAN's body. The
YOUNG MAN rushes to a lever under the lift and pulls it.
Nothing happens. He yanks it to the right and left. Nothing
happens. He kicks the lever. Still nothing.*

YOUNG MAN

Come on, come on! Work, mother fucker! Work! Why
won't you work! Work! Please work! Please! Pretty
please! Work. Oh work! Please work! Work! Work!
Work! Work! Work!

*Sound of bell in gas station and car pulling up and stop-
ping off left. The YOUNG MAN runs off right leaving the
car up on the rack. Sound of jet passing overhead. Silence.
A man is heard whistling off left.*

VOICE

Shorty! Anybody home?

A FOREST RANGER comes on from left, dressed in uniform and sipping a Coke. He just wanders onstage without seeing the bodies and glancing up at the car.

BLACKOUT

"Pipeline" by the HOLY MODAL ROUNDERS comes on in the dark.

OPERATION SIDEWINDER
music by HOLY MODAL ROUNDERS

FLOAT ME DOWN YOUR PIPELINE

Float me down your pipeline sometime
I came here with my guidebook
With my license in hand
But the landing field keeps slipping out of line
And this ain't what they told me I'd find
The biggest laugh around here
Is the changing ground here
Down in the alley
When the game gets fast
There ain't no piece of paper
Gonna save your ass
So float me down your pipeline sometime

I need to find a guideline sometime
These old concentric circles
Are spinning me out
And everything I do goes down in doubt
So won't you show me which way is out
I guess this is the moment
When I might need a friend
Backwater waiting for my mind to break
Guess you're the only chance that's left to take
So float me down your pipeline sometime.

by ANTONIA

SCENE 3

The song fades into the sound of the sidewinder's rattle. The blinking red eyes are seen in the dark.

The lights come up on BILLY, an old prospector with a long gray beard, floppy hat, yellow shirt, red bandana, overalls with suspenders, long boots, pots and pans attached to his waist so they clang when he walks, and a pack on the floor beside him. He is sitting on his haunches directly behind HONEY who is lying frozen in the same position with the snake coiled around her body. BILLY talks to her in a calm soothing voice. The snake continues its rhythms.

BILLY

Well, that was just about nineteen–o–six when they was a' gettin' all het up about the area. Yep. If you'd a told any one a' them ten thousand folks back then that their boom town weren't a gonna have nothin' left but a shanty and some wild burros come nineteen–seventy–one, why there wouldn't a' been a one of 'em would a paid ya' no never mind. No sir. They smelled that gold pumpin' through the rhyolite and there weren't no one gonna stop that town from boomin'. 'Course there's still a few old tough ones like myself and Death Valley Smiley and Wheelburro Tex and Dapper Tommy Thompson and some a the others. Still loco enough to believe them old yarns.

HONEY makes a low groaning sound and starts to undulate with the sidewinder. She seems to get more and more turned on as BILLY tries to calm her.

19

BILLY

> Now, ya' don't want to move around much there, Miss. I've seen these here critters strike so fast it'd make yer head swim. 'Course now this one's a bit extra sized. Can't say fer certain when I ever did see such a big one. If it weren't the middle of the American desert here I'd even be prone to say she was a boa constrictor. Like they have in Africa and such. 'Course that's a tad far fetched. Never can tell though. Them Air Force boys pull some mighty funny stunts out here. There's a bunch of 'em stationed just close by here ya' know. Over at Fort George. Maybe you seen 'em roarin' by. Roarin' by. Testin' the sky fer holes or somethin'. Nothin' else to do. Could be one a them fellas dropped this big feller right out a' the sky. Ain't likely. I mean, first off they'd have to fly off to Africa to get the damned thing in the first place. Then fly it back out here. Ain't likely. Could just be though. They get so gall-darned bored I'll betcha'. Testin' all the time. Sure. Nothin' else to do but fly around makin' explosions. Droppin' snakes. Probably think it's funny. Get a big charge outa' trappin' young ladies. I'll betcha'.

HONEY has an orgasm as the YOUNG MAN comes running on from right. BILLY smiles and stands up, his arms outstretched. The YOUNG MAN crosses down left paying no attention to HONEY or the sidewinder.

BILLY

> Jimmy boy! Right on time. Just like clock work. Look what I found here, Danny. Just lyin' here while I was a waitin'. Come by to wait and here she was, all bound up and chokin' to death. So I tried to tell her a thing or two about the desert and snakes and such.

YOUNG MAN
Come here, Billy.

BILLY
What ya' got there, Johnny? I been a' waitin' like ya' told me. I don't ferget.

BILLY crosses down to the YOUNG MAN who takes out the gun and runs his hands over it. The YOUNG MAN turns to BILLY and holds out the gun for him to see. BILLY takes it.

BILLY
Oh, now Jimmy, ya' shore got a nice one. Ya' needn't a' got such a nice rod fer that half breed. He don't know the difference 'tween a B.B. gun and a thirty–odd–six.

YOUNG MAN
I want him to have this one. You'll see that he gets it, Billy?

BILLY
Shore. I'll hand it right over. No trouble 'tall.

YOUNG MAN
Now listen carefully. I've run into some trouble so I'm going to have to do some doubling back. Now tell Mickey Free to meet me right here tomorrow at sunrise. You got that?

BILLY
Sunrise tomorrow.

YOUNG MAN

Right. Now tell him to come alone and not to bring the gun. I'll explain the rest when he gets here.

BILLY

Alone and no iron. I savvy, Johnny.

YOUNG MAN

O.K. Now get going.

BILLY

What about the lady?

YOUNG MAN

What lady?

BILLY motions to HONEY who again has become rigid as the sidewinder blinks and spits and rattles.

She's got nothing to do with me. Now get going and remember what I just told you.

BILLY

O.K., Danny. Adios!

The YOUNG MAN hurries off right. BILLY walks up to HONEY and around behind her. He picks up his pack and slings it over his shoulder. He bends over and looks into HONEY's face. Her eyes are into a blank stare. BILLY shakes his head and goes off left twirling the pistol and singing softly.

"A beautiful bird in a gilded cage.
A beautiful sight to see.

You may think she's happy and free from fear.
She ain't though she seems to be."

The lights fade to BLACKOUT as BILLY exits.

"Generalonely" is heard in the BLACKOUT.

OPERATION SIDEWINDER
music by HOLY MODAL ROUNDERS

GENERALONELY

Sad news has come to town, the blues it came in
Right up through my front door, looked like it was staying
My aide de camp replied, "What's that it's saying"
The blues has come to town looks like it's staying

A General am I and a General only
Generally I'm generally lonely
A General am I and a General only
Generally I'm generally lonely

Generally I'm generally lonely
Generally but a General only
Then my aide de camp replied, "The legal tenderly
And now we are all registered blues members"

by STEVE WEBER

SCENE 4

The song fades out as the lights come up on an Air Force COLONEL seated behind his desk with a glass of brandy and a cigar, his foot up on the desk. Across from him is a CAPTAIN, also sipping brandy but slightly drunker than the COLONEL. Behind them is a huge colorful map of the U.S. An American eagle. Photographs of jets in flight. Trophies on the desk.

COLONEL

Trouble with that bitch was, you just didn't get her out in the world enough, Henry. A young bitch like that's gotta come in contact with a whole lotta people and noise. Otherwise you'll just never get her cured. There's a world of difference between your dog and your bitch. A lot of breeders forget that. Just like people. Now a woman's just naturally gonna' be more sensitive than a man. No two ways about it. Same with a dog.

CAPTAIN

I don't know about that, Warner. I've seen some pretty spookey males in my day.

COLONEL

Sure! You're gonna get your share of gun shy males too. No way around it. That's that old argument. That heredity and environment thing. I wouldn't be the one to take sides for either. They both got their strong points. But I'll tell you this much. You can't expect a young pup, male or female, to grow up into a healthy bird dog if he's had a bad surrounding when he was little. Like a pup who's been around a lot of little brats pestering him all the time and making loud noises right in his ear. He's not gonna grow up as brave as the pup who had a quiet peaceful home. Have some more brandy, Henry.

CAPTAIN
No. No thanks.

COLONEL
Aw, go on. Don't cost me nothin'.

CAPTAIN
All right.

The COLONEL pours him another drink.

Say, Warner, you know that big stud dog you got? The one with the speckled chest?

COLONEL
Bruce. Sure. Oh no. I'm reading your mind right now, Captain.

CAPTAIN
What?

COLONEL
I suppose you want to breed that gun shy bitch of yours to my male.

CAPTAIN
Well her conformation makes up for her tempera-

ment. You gotta admit that much. She's got one of the best heads you'll see in a long time.

COLONEL

A pretty head don't mean she can smell birds. Some of the best hunting dogs I've seen have been ugly as sin. Now come on, Henry. You don't want my Bruce to go getting a trauma right off the bat. He's only sired two litters so far, and if she gives him a bad bite he might never get over it. I mean I gotta think of his future too.

CAPTAIN

She's not gonna go biting your male, Warner. Besides, we could muzzle her.

COLONEL

Oh no. Absolutely not! I never muzzled a dog in my life and I never will. I don't care if it's the meanest dog around. That's something you just don't do to an animal. I saw a dog almost suffocate on its own saliva once. Just from that very same thing.

CAPTAIN

Well we wouldn't go off and leave them alone. I'd stand right there and hold her.

COLONEL

I'm sorry, Henry. It's just not the way I like to breed my dogs. It's a very touchy game. You're dealing with living animals, not machines.

A loud knock on the door.

Come in!

A CADET enters and salutes stiffly.

At ease.

CADET
> Colonel, sir. Your presence is requested immediately at the laboratory, sir. It seems the sidewinder computer has escaped.

The COLONEL stands abruptly, knocking over his brandy glass. The CAPTAIN tries to get out of his seat but he's too drunk.

COLONEL
> Escaped! What do you mean escaped! It's under strict surveillance!

CADET
> I'm not sure, sir. That was the message from General Browser, sir.

COLONEL
> How could a computer escape? Answer me that!

CADET
> I have no idea, sir. That was the whole message, sir. General Browser and Dr. Vector are waiting in the lab, sir.

COLONEL
> Tell them I'm on my way. Go on!

CADET
> Yes sir!

The CADET salutes and exits.

COLONEL
Of all the goddamned nerve! Escaped!

BLACKOUT

"Catch Me" comes on in the dark.

OPERATION SIDEWINDER
music by HOLY MODAL ROUNDERS

CATCH ME

Catch me if you can while I last 'cause there's nothin' to
    keep me around
Touch me with a ten foot pole and I'll make both your feet
    leave the ground
Watch me if you can't come along 'cause I got enough here
    for us both
It's eating me inside out but I know that it won't stunt my
    growth

It doesn't matter what you try it's all about take and give
It doesn't matter how you die but only how you iive

I'm burning up ninety-nine pounds of rubber up here in the
    sky
I don't know just how I got wheels or why it's so easy to fly
I can't see for millions of miles it looks like a fog up ahead
Catch me if I crash to the ground and make sure I don't land
    on my head

It doesn't matter what you try it's all about take and give
It doesn't matter how you die but only how you live

by SAM SHEPARD

SCENE 5

*The song fades into the rattle of the sidewinder. The blink-
ing red eyes. Hissing. The lights come up on HONEY, still
entangled by the sidewinder.*

*Three men are standing behind her, watching the side-
winder intently. MICKEY FREE is in the middle with two
Apache INDIANS standing slightly behind him, one on either side. All three have long flowing black hair which falls
down over their shoulders.*

*The two INDIANS are very dark skinned and dressed in the
renegade Apache costume of the late eighteen hundreds,
but unique from each other. Knee length moccasin boots,
rawhide pants, long loin cloths with Mexican type designs, heavy shirts, suit jackets captured from wayward
whites, tooth and bone necklaces, straight brimmed black
hats with Mexican silver coin headbands, two wide belts of
ammunition criss-crossing from shoulder to waist, knives
sticking out of the tops of their moccasins and 30.30 rifles
from the cavalry times.*

*MICKEY FREE is a half breed: Mexican, Irish, Apache; his
skin is lighter but he looks Indian. He's half blind in his
right eye so he squints it constantly and moves his head
in strange ways. He is dressed like the Apaches but flash-
ier in spots and more heavily armed. His prize weapon is a
huge Bowie knife with a turquoise and silver handle which
he keeps in a beaded deerskin sheath which hangs down
over his crotch, like a cock piece.*

*All three of them watch HONEY and the sidewinder in si-
lence as she goes through throes of agony-ecstasy with the*

sidewinder continuing his relentless moves and rhythms. Finally her eyes open and she looks up at MICKEY FREE.

HONEY

Help me.

The INDIANS are silent. MICKEY FREE stares at her with his one good eye.

Please. Help me.

MICKEY turns to the INDIANS. The INDIANS speak to him in Apache. The language should sound like a mixture of Spanish and Oriental.

1ST INDIAN

Natcha la oot. Gracha om laate.

2ND INDIAN

No me ta santo. Este un gran mal muerta.

MICKEY FREE is silent. He turns back to HONEY and looks down at her.

HONEY

Please, help me. Please. Help me.

MICKEY takes out his huge Bowie knife and kneels down beside HONEY. He strokes the head of the sidewinder with his left hand very gently and makes a soothing sound in his throat. Suddenly his left hand seizes the neck of the sidewinder and squeezes it. The jaws pop open revealing huge fangs.

He makes one sudden slash with the knife and the head comes off, leaving the body writhing and squirming on

HONEY, who screams and goes into hysteria. She flings the body downstage and collapses. The body writhes as MICKEY slowly stands up still holding the head with the eyes still blinking.

The INDIANS make sounds of approval and touch the snake's head. MICKEY smiles and wipes the knife off on his pants then puts it back in the sheath. He drops the head into a beaded pouch which he wears on his waist. The body stops writhing. The VOICE of the YOUNG MAN is heard off right.

YOUNG MAN'S VOICE
Mickey? That you, Mickey?

MICKEY and the INDIANS look off right. HONEY is in delirium daze.

HONEY
Dukie?

The YOUNG MAN comes on from right.

YOUNG MAN
Mickey! You made it!

He looks at HONEY.

I see you're free now. Why don't you split.

HONEY looks bewildered. The YOUNG MAN moves center downstage, MICKEY follows with the INDIANS close behind. The YOUNG MAN takes two plasticene bags filled with white powder out of his crotch and sets them on the ground. He sits down cross-legged. MICKEY sits beside him with the bags between them. The INDIANS stand behind.

YOUNG MAN
> Did Billy give you the gun?

MICKEY
> Yes.

YOUNG MAN
> Is it all right?

MICKEY
> Yes.

YOUNG MAN
> Good. Now——

MICKEY
> I'll need more than one gun.

YOUNG MAN
> O.K. I'll see what I can do. How many do you want?

MICKEY
> Two more.

YOUNG MAN
> O.K. I'll get them by next week. How's that?

MICKEY
> Good. Give them to Billy. He give them to me.

YOUNG MAN
> Yeah. Now . . . .

MICKEY
> You have a ready roll?

YOUNG MAN   **1545048**

Sure.

He takes out a cigarette and hands it to MICKEY.

MICKEY

You have two more?

The YOUNG MAN offers the pack to the two INDIANS.

YOUNG MAN

Here. Keep the pack.

The INDIANS take the pack and take out cigarettes. MICKEY puts out his hand to the INDIANS. They give the pack to MICKEY who puts it in the top of his moccasin. MICKEY takes out a butane lighter from his other moccasin and lights his cigarette, then he lights the INDIANS'.

YOUNG MAN

Now, this is the stuff. It's more than enough to do the trick.

MICKEY

Trick?

YOUNG MAN

Yeah. Trick, job.

MICKEY

Job.

YOUNG MAN

Now your job is very easy but you have to pull it off without fail. There's a lot of people counting on you. People you've never seen before. You're going to mean a lot to them if everything works the way we have it run down. Now the reason we've come to you is because you know the layout of Fort George probably better than anyone in the desert, mainly because you helped them get it started.

MICKEY

Yes. I find them low ground.

YOUNG MAN

Right. And that's valuable to us because now you can take these bags directly to their reservoir and dump them without anyone getting suspicious. Now here's the plan: tomorrow, you and your friends ride into the fort at high noon. You go straight to the commanding officer's headquarters and ask to speak to General Browser. They'll ask you what you want to see him about and you tell them that you're looking for work.

MICKEY

Work!

YOUNG MAN

Yeah. Work, job. You need a job. And then they'll tell you they're very sorry but they have no work, come back some other time, and you say all right and start to leave. Then you ask them if it's all right if you water your horses out at the reservoir because you've been riding all day and they're really wiped out. Then they'll probably give you a pass to enter the reservoir area. If they don't then ask them for one. Then you take the pass, get back on your horses, with the dope in your saddle bags.

MICKEY
        Dope?

YOUNG MAN
        Yeah, the stuff! And ride into the reservoir area. I
        doubt if they'll have a guard on duty there but if they
        do I'm sure you can handle him. Just show him the
        pass and play dumb. When you get to the reservoir,
        dismount and water your horses. Then just take the
        dope out of the saddle bags and cut the bags open
        and let all the powder fall into the water. Be sure to
        put the empty plastic bags back in your saddle bags.
        Don't leave them at the reservoir. Then just get back
        on your horse and ride away. You got it?

MICKEY
        Yes.

YOUNG MAN
        Good.

MICKEY
        I have more friends who wish to help too. They say
        anything that will make the silver birds leave the
        skies will be pleasing to the Spider Woman.

YOUNG MAN
        Tell them to wait. Anything can happen. We'll let
        them know.

        MICKEY gives an order to the INDIANS.

MICKEY
        Nanza nienta paz. Para los caballos.

*The INDIANS go to the plasticene bags. One of them has a
leather saddle bag which he opens while the other one puts
the bags inside. MICKEY stands up with the YOUNG MAN.
They shake hands by clasping each other's wrists.*

YOUNG MAN
I'll come to your place next week and let you know
how things went.

MICKEY
Good.

YOUNG MAN
Good luck.

MICKEY
Hasta luego.

*The three of them go offstage left. The YOUNG MAN looks
at HONEY who is staring at him with a blank gaze.*

YOUNG MAN
What're you looking at?

*He reaches into his pocket and pulls out a small leather
pouch with a zipper. He sits down and zips it open. He
takes out a needle, an eye dropper syringe and a small vial
of liquid. He lifts up his T shirt and feels for his belt. He
notices he's not wearing one.*

Hey! Do you have a belt on you? Or a tie?

HONEY
Belt? No.

He looks around the stage angrily. He sees the sidewind-

er's body. He reaches for it and grabs the rattle end, pull-
ing it close to him. He fixes up the needle, opens the vial
and draws the liquid up into the syringe.

Do you have any water?

YOUNG MAN
Yeah. It's in the canteen.

HONEY scrambles to the canteen, opens it and takes a
long drink. The YOUNG MAN struggles with the snake's
body, trying to tie it as a tourniquet around his left arm.

HONEY
What are you doing?

YOUNG MAN
Trying to get off. What does it look like. Fuck! Would
you come here for a second.

HONEY
What?

YOUNG MAN
Just come here. I'm not going to bite you.

HONEY crawls to him on her hands and knees.

Would you wrap this tight around my arm and just
hold it.

HONEY
Are you crazy? That thing almost strangled me to
death.

YOUNG MAN

Well now it's your turn to strangle it. Come on. Look. He's dead.

He shakes the sidewinder's body in her face. She jumps back.

Dead! Just do it for a favor. O.K.? Please? Come on. Be a sport.

She takes the snake and wraps it around his left arm.

Pull. Now just hold on to it. Don't let go.

HONEY pulls the snake tight. The YOUNG MAN rubs his vein and jabs the needle in. HONEY makes a shriek and jumps back, letting the snake go. The YOUNG MAN lets out a yell.

Oh fuck! You stupid cunt! You almost broke my point! My last point! You almost ripped out my vein! Jesus Christ!

He rubs his arm in agony.

HONEY

I'm sorry. I didn't know you were gonna poke yourself.

YOUNG MAN

I told you not to let go. Now would you wrap it tight and hold on this time.

HONEY

All right.

She goes through the same thing again with the snake. He jabs the needle in this time and gets a hit.

YOUNG MAN

All right. Now let go slowly. Slowly. Easy. That's it.

She slowly releases her grip on the sidewinder. It falls to the floor. The YOUNG MAN relaxes and smiles at HONEY.

Now. That wasn't so bad, was it?

HONEY

Are you a diabetic?

YOUNG MAN

Yeah. I need lots of sugar.

HONEY

Could I have some?

YOUNG MAN

You think you need it?

HONEY

I can't seem to get up any energy. I mean you use it for energy, don't you? That darn snake knocked the wind out of me.

YOUNG MAN

I suppose I could spare some. Just to get you up on your feet. Don't come asking me for more though.

HONEY

Oh, I won't. I just need a boost. Boy, I'm really glad you came along. You know? I thought I was gonna be stuck out here forever. There's a lot of creepy people out here. You're the first decent person I've seen.

He wraps the snake around her right arm.

YOUNG MAN

All right. Now grab both ends and pull tight. Close your eyes and don't look. O.K.?

She follows his orders as the YOUNG MAN fills the syringe and HONEY talks with her eyes closed. The lights fade out to BLACK as the YOUNG MAN shoots her up.

HONEY

It's not going to hurt, is it? I've had enough pain for one day. I just have to get up enough energy to look for Dukie. He's my husband. He just all of a sudden ran off some place to get some help and I haven't seen him since. We were on our way to Las Vegas to get a divorce. It's not that we weren't happy or anything. We were very happy. We just needed a change you know. A sort of a vacation from each other. So we decided to make it a vacation together. You know what I mean. I mean so long as we were getting divorced we might as well make it a vacation. Kill two birds with one stone. Then this snake got me and I don't even know what happened. One minute we were together and the next minute we were separated. Just like that. I guess this desert does funny things to your brain or something. It's not going to hurt me, is it?

BLACKOUT

HONEY screams. "Euphoria" is heard in the dark.

OPERATION SIDEWINDER
music by HOLY MODAL ROUNDERS

EUPHORIA

Ma's out here switchin' in the kitchen
And dad's in the living room grousin' and a bitchin'
And I'm out here kicking the gong for "Euphoria"

Euphoria when your mind goes wheelin' and a walkin'
Your inside voices go squealin' and a squawkin'
Floating around on a belladonna cloud
Singing Euphoria

There's a man in the corner underneath a table
He sat makin' faces at a union label
He pitched his ears and then he rolled his eyes
And whispered "Euphoria"

Euphoria when your mind goes wheelin' and a walkin'
Your inside voices go squealin' and a squawkin'
Floating around on a belladonna cloud
Singing Euphoria

I went for a walk and just got back
I saw a junkie mother boosting Similac
She had her baby on her back and her works in her hand
She hollered "Euphoria"

Euphoria when your mind goes wheelin' and a walkin'
Your inside voices go squealin' and a squawkin'
Floating around on a belladonna cloud
Singing Euphoria

Pinched Eve on the bottom, patted Adam on the back
Smiled at the serpent and it winked back
Took a bite from the apple with two bites gone
And hollered "Euphoria"

Euphoria when your mind goes wheelin' and a walkin'
Your inside voices go squealin' and a squawkin'
Floating around on a belladonna cloud
Singing Euphoria

by ROBIN REMAILY

SCENE 6

The song fades out. The lights slowly come up on a '57 Chevy convertible. Three Blacks are sitting in the car. BLOOD is driving. BLADE and DUDE sit in the back. Above them hanging in mid air is a huge hot dog sign. A CARHOP enters from left and walks up to the car. She is young and dressed in a stupid white mini outfit with a funny hat, a check book and pencil.

CARHOP
Can I help you guys?

BLOOD

To the two in back.

What do you want?

BLADE
Let me have a cheeseburger, a chocolate malt and a order a fries.

DUDE
Yeah. Same thing for me except make it vanilla.

CARHOP
The malt?

BLADE
Right.

CARHOP
Say, are you guys with the Panthers?

DUDE
No, we're with the Rams.

BLOOD
Let me have a B.L.T. on whole wheat toast with mayo.

CARHOP
A B.L.T. on whole wheat.

BLOOD
And a large milk.

CARHOP
Sure. You know I've been wanting to talk to some of your people for a long time. I go to City College and it seems like there's this whole huge gap in dialogue between what we're trying to do and what you're trying to do. You know what I mean? Like I can really dig this whole unity thing that you guys are into but it seems like we could be doing something to help bind it all together. You know. I mean you people have such a groovy thing going.

BLOOD
Yeah, right.

CARHOP
I mean all this shit about the pigs man. I mean fuck the pigs. Forget all those gray people. We're not going to turn on any of those zombies. We gotta find our own people. Turn ourselves on. Make something happen for us.

DUDE

For us?

CARHOP

Yeah, us. You and me. Fuck them. All that festering bullshit is just going to collapse anyway. I mean I gotta work to pay for my school but once that's over man, I'm gone. You know? I mean I'm going to go out and help organize, help get it together. Because if we don't get it together pretty soon we're gonna be had. Am I right?

BLADE

Right.

CARHOP

And I'm not just doing a rap to make myself feel good either. Because I got nothing to lose. Least of all this shitty job. I mean I can see where things are at. With you guys it's all laid out. With me it's different. I got a lot of guessing to do. With you it's armed struggle. I'm for that. I think it's a necessary step. A revolution begins when a faction seizes power and begins to use it to change society. Armed struggle comes before the revolution. Armed struggle begins when the oppressed people pick up guns and are willing to die for the revolution. I'm willing. I know you guys are. I got a gun right in my house man and I'm ready to use it too.

BLOOD

Good. What kind is it?

CARHOP

What? The gun? I'm not sure. A thirty-eight or some-

thing. But listen, we can't afford to compromise anymore. Some people are saying all they want is a
piece of the American pie. Well we can't have a piece
of that pie because that pie exploits our brothers in
Vietnam, in Latin America and in Africa.

BLOOD

Let me have a piece of cherry pie with that too.

CARHOP

Cherry pie?

BLOOD

Yeah. With the B.L.T.

CARHOP

Oh. O.K. All right. One cherry pie. Right. I'll be right
back.

She writes it down on her check book and exits right.

BLOOD

Now, down to business.

DUDE

Yeah, what's the story with this flower child in the
desert? You really trust him to deliver the goods?

BLOOD

Don't worry, once that dope takes hold the Air Force
is going to be doing some mighty funny things.

BLADE

How's it supposed to work anyway?

BLOOD

    Mickey Free makes the drop. Right?

BLADE

    Right.

BLOOD

    The pilots get a good taste of supersonic water. They start feeling funny. They hear voices. They see things in the air. They hear music. They get stoned like they never been before in their lives.

DUDE

    Then what?

BLOOD

    In the middle of the night they all get up in unison like Dracula and his sisters and walk straight out into the night. They climb into their sleek super duper F-one-elevens and take off. They fly straight for a little island just south of Miami whereupon they land and await further instructions.

DUDE

    Sounds pretty shaky to me.

BLOOD

    How come?

DUDE

    I don't know, it's like James Bond or something. Why don't we just go in and take the thing over.

BLADE

    Yeah, I can't see getting involved with this hippie cat Blood. His mind's been burned out. The drug thing just isn't going to pull it off.

BLOOD

We gotta give it some time. It's just a step.

DUDE

Watch it, here comes the S.D.S.

The CARHOP enters again with their order. She walks up to them.

CARHOP

Say listen I'm sorry I got so carried away before but I really meant what I said.

BLOOD

Right. You got the milk?

CARHOP

Milk? Oh. Yeah. Here it is. I mean we can't debate whether we want revolution or whether we don't want revolution because for our survival we're going to have to make revolution. Right? I mean I guess you guys already know that.

BLADE

Pass the french fries.

BLACKOUT

"Synergy" is heard.

OPERATION SIDEWINDER
music by HOLY MODAL ROUNDERS

SYNERGY

CHORUS:
> Superman's on the can contemplating synergy
> Lone ranger on the range and Dr. Strange got synergy
> Cool heads certainly agree concerning synergy
> Likewise Liberace's momma
> Donald Duck and Dalai Lama
> Yes sir!

Come along, sing with me sing a song of synergy
Find that peace in your soul
We're all one and heaven is our goal

> CHORUS

Synergy will get us all and it's going to be a ball
Kick that gong, ring that bell, synergy will save us all from
hell

> CHORUS

Be a friend, lend a hand, try your best to understand
We are all born alone, but the light of love can lead us home

> CHORUS

Get undressed, plant a tree, make love to machinery
Throw away all the locks, open up the jails and stop the
clocks

> CHORUS

We can have paradise right now at a bargain price
Heaven is ours to make, peace on earth is there for us to take

> CHORUS

by PETER STAMPFEL & ANTONIA

SCENE 7

The Air Force Laboratory at Fort George. Test tubes, vials, bunsen burners, a general clutter of chemical and electronic gadgets. In the middle of all this is DOCTOR VECTOR, sitting in a wheelchair, dressed in a white chemist's smock. He is very tiny and his entire body is twisted and bent. He wears extra thick dark glasses and elevator shoes and speaks with a weird shifting accent. When he wants to move his wheelchair he presses a button on one of the arms and the chair propels itself electronically. On either side of him are GENERAL BROWSER, obviously pissed off but trying to keep his cool, and COLONEL WARNER who goes into fits of temper but snaps out of it by the GENERAL's presence.

COLONEL

I've never in my whole career in the United States Air Force heard of such a half cocked idea as this one! I mean freedom to experiment to my mind has always meant for the experimenter, I mean the person or persons doing the experiment, not the goddamn experiment itself! Now that's just never ever been done before, Doctor Vector, and I for one . . . .

GENERAL

Now settle down, Warner. I'm sure the doctor had his reasons for allowing this to happen. What's done is done. The fact is that I should have personally seen to it that the arrangements for Operation Sidewinder were made more clear to everyone involved. Including myself. I certainly had no idea you were off on a tangent like this, Doctor Vector.

DR. VECTOR

What tangent? No tangent. This now is marking the beginning of the stage I had so long awaited. You should both be beaming with the joy I now feel. The sidewinder computer has now chosen to go off on its own accord. It has chosen to be free and exist on its own. For weeks I have watched it writhing and squirming with its wonderful powerful body. Sidewinding its way around its little artificial desert. Searching for a way out. Searching every corner. Its magnificent head straining toward the top of the glass then back down to the bottom. Knowing that all around, outside, out in the real world was a desert and sky so vast and so free. A captive with more cosmic secrets than a man could learn from the whole of history. Finally I saw the decision lay in my hands, gentlemen. In my hands. It was up to me to either keep this creature in its cage and continue to feed it my steady diet of limited knowledge or to set it free and have it discover its true potential. Do you realize the magnitude of this action? It means for the first time ever we can begin to study the effects of the machine's own decisions on its own survival. For the first time in history we shall see if it is possible to produce a machine with its own brain and its own synthetic form of life and have it survive on its own without our constant presence and supervision. All this and still have it retain the willingness to achieve the purpose for which it was programmed. Oh sure, you say it's already been done before. Some biochemist in New Jersey might be maybe come up with some small germ of plastic bacteria that he says is life. All year they watch it under glass and give it injections and change the light and switch around

the soils but so what! That is no experiment! Not like the sidewinder! The sidewinder computer this very minute is surviving on one of the most inhospitable deserts in the world! Surviving by its own synthetic wits! And you two talk as though we have thrown away a lifetime! Bah! The Army should never have nothing to do with Science!

COLONEL

This is the Air Force, Doctor! And it's not a lifetime that you've thrown away but almost two billion dollars! How does that grab you?

GENERAL

Now wait a minute, Colonel. The Doctor seems to feel that his sidewinder computer will perform better and reveal more information to us if left on its own. That's all well and good. However, I'm left with certain uncertainties, Doctor.

DR. VECTOR

Yah, General?

GENERAL

From a purely pragmatic point of view, now that the computer has escaped, or in your words ventured off on its own, how is it possible for you to program it or even trace its existence, if in fact it is still alive. I mean . . . .

COLONEL

Alive! Judas Priest!

DR. VECTOR

Gentlemen, gentlemen! Operation Sidewinder was

begun by the government in late 1964 Yah? (Yah!) in an effort to produce a tracing computer which would help to solve the questions of whether or not unidentified flying objects actually existed. Oui? (Oui!) Since that time we have discovered that they do in fact exist Dah? (Dah) and the next step, as you both are well aware, was of course to trace their flight patterns in an effort to learn their trade routes and possibly the planet or star from where they are living.

COLONEL

Now come off it, Doc. We all know that Constellation Pegasus has . . . .

GENERAL

Please, Colonel! Let the Doctor finish.

DR. VECTOR

At this stage it became apparent to me that all man made efforts to produce this type of information were useless and that a much more sophisticated form of intelligence was necessary. A form of intelligence which, being triggered from the mind of man, would eventually, if allowed to exist on its own, transcend the barriers of human thought and penetrate an extraterrestrial consciousness. This is when I began my studies of the Western rattlesnakes and experimenting with the possibilities of their rhythmic movements being directly connected with the movements of the planets and the flight patterns of the UFO's. These studies resulted in the initial design for my sidewinder computer. Now, whether or not the sidewinder will be able to attain this realm of extraterrestrial consciousness is something none of us will know until we are ready. One thing is for certain, the sidewinder must have complete freedom to discover this realm for itself. And gentlemen, if it succeeds we will be the first to know. Think of it, gentlemen! We will be in direct contact with these flying objects and eventually with those who operate and control them!

COLONEL

What a bunch a' horse shit!

BLACKOUT

"Dusty Fustchuns" comes on in the dark.

OPERATION SIDEWINDER
music by HOLY MODAL ROUNDERS

"DUSTY FUSTCHUNS"

Don't leave me dying in the desert
Don't leave me dangling in the dust
I don't wanna live here with these here lizards
They look at me with a cold and hungry lust
Big bird circlin' in the sky is a buzzard
Think he got his eye on me
The ever shiftin sand is the only sound I hear
And that mirage over there is the only water near

I got a pound of sand in my navel
When night comes I turn into ice
At high noon brains melt like butter
No one to talk to but the toads and the mice

Devil take away these damn sand dunes
Devil take away this sun
Devil take away this dry dusty hole
This is all a mistake and
I'm cooked 'til overdone

(Coyote howls for last verse)

by ROBIN REMAILY

SCENE 8

The song fades into the sound of crickets. A coyote howls. A full moon glows in the dark. Stars come out. The lights fade up slowly to bluish moonlight.

The YOUNG MAN and HONEY are lying on their backs up- stage staring at the night sky. The body of the sidewinder is downstage left. HONEY moves voluptuously around on her back, stretching and unbuttoning her blouse. The YOUNG MAN just stares at the sky.

HONEY

Oh, it's so gorgeous. A full moon. And the stars. I never felt so good in my whole life. Everything smells so wild out here. Smell the yucca. It's so peaceful and nice. Hey, what's your name anyway? Do you have a name? My name's Honey. That's because my husband called me that. He said it was because of my honey hair. My yellow honey hair. Dukie said it even smelled like honey. You wanna' smell my hair? You can smell it if you want. Sometimes I even smell it. I used to all the time. When I was a little girl. I'd go in the closet and smell it. I never cut it because my Mama said that sometime . . . someday I'd make my living from my hair. That's what she told me. That I should come to Hollywood and the very next day, just from walking around the streets and every- thing, that someone would see my hair and ask me to come and get a screen test. And that before very long I'd be famous and rich and everything. I'd never have to worry about a man supporting me or any-

thing because I'd have enough to support myself.
And then I met Dukie and . . . .

*A shock of blue light goes off above the stage, like a huge
flash bulb. Then a beam of white light goes across the sky
behind them from left to right and disappears. HONEY sits
up. The YOUNG MAN stays relaxed on his back. HONEY
stares up at the sky.*

HONEY

Hey! Did you see that!

YOUNG MAN

Shooting stars.

HONEY

Boy. I never saw one before. It looks like it's still
there.

YOUNG MAN

Why should it go away?

HONEY

Well, don't they just fall and then . . . Look! Look at
the way it's moving. Sideways. I'm scared.

YOUNG MAN

Why be scared of a star?

HONEY

What if it's not a star? What if it's one of those creepy
saucer things?

YOUNG MAN

What if it is?

HONEY

Boy, you don't get very excited about anything, do you?

She lies back down next to the YOUNG MAN moving closer and trying to turn him on.

YOUNG MAN

Only when it counts.

HONEY

I'll bet you're really something when you get excited. How come you don't get a haircut?

YOUNG MAN

'Cause my Pappy told me that one day I'd make my living from my hair.

HONEY

Are you making fun of me?

YOUNG MAN

No. It's true. My Pappy was way ahead of his time. He said, son, in a few years all a young man'll have to do to make a few bucks is just grow his hair long and set on a street corner and things'll just start happening to him. Like magic.

HONEY

Do you believe in magic?

YOUNG MAN

I used to. I walked through the crowd. I saw my best friends there. Real friends. I felt such a warm bond between us. Like we were all in the same place at the same time for the same reason.

HONEY
What are you talking about?

YOUNG MAN
And suddenly I felt free, my mind was lifting up, up, up in flight. Not like that thirteen year old wild, crazy, out of the house on Friday night feeling but something much deeper. Like nothing could hurt me. Nothing could touch my peace.

HONEY
Boy, you're really weird.

YOUNG MAN
It was like all that oppression from the month before had suddenly cracked open and left me in space. The election oppression: Nixon, Wallace, Humphrey. The headline oppression every morning with one of their names on it. The radio news broadcast, TV oppression. And every other advertisement with their names and faces and voices and haircuts and suits and collars and ties and lies. And I was all set to watch "Mission: Impossible" when Humphrey's flabby face shows up for another hour's alienation session. Oh please say something kind to us, something soft, something human, something different, something real, something—so we can believe again. His squirmy little voice answers me, "You can't always have everything your way." And the oppression of my fellow students becoming depressed. Depressed. Despaired. Running out of gas. "We're not going to win. There's nothing we can do to win." This is how it be-

gins, I see. We become so depressed we don't fight anymore. We're only losing a little, we say. It could be so much worse. The soldiers are dying, the Blacks are dying, the children are dying. It could be so much worse. Everything must be considered in light of the political situation. No getting around it. It could be so much worse.

HONEY

Think about something nice.

YOUNG MAN

Let's wait till four years from now when we can take over the Democratic Party. Teddy Kennedy is still alive. Let's not do anything at all. It can only get worse. Let's give up. And then I walked through the crowd of smiling people. They were loving and happy, alive and free. You can't win all the time. You can't always have everything your own way. You'll be arrested. You'll be arrested, accosted, molested, tested and re-tested. You'll be beaten, you'll be jailed, you'll be thrown out of school. You'll be spanked, you'll be whipped and chained. But I am whipped. I am chained. I am prisoner to all your oppression. I am depressed, deranged, decapitated, dehumanized, defoliated, demented and damned! I can't get out. You can get out. You can smile and laugh and kiss and cry. I am! I am! I am! I am! I am! I am! I am! I am! I am! I am! I am! Tonight. In this desert. In this space. I am.

Another flash of blue light that seems more prolonged this time. Again the beam of light goes across the sky from stage left to stage right. At the same time the body of the sidewinder lights up green and jumps. The rattle rattles and the end of the tail begins to twitch. HONEY screams and cuddles close to the YOUNG MAN who sits up slightly.

YOUNG MAN

What's the matter now?

HONEY

That snake! It's still alive! It moved!

YOUNG MAN

Bullshit.

HONEY

It did! It lit up green and moved. There! Look at it! It twitched! Didn't you see it!

YOUNG MAN

You're just hallucinating. Relax.

HONEY

I swear it moved. Listen! Can't you hear it? It's rattling. It's still alive! Sit up and look at it!

The YOUNG MAN lies on his back and stares at the sky. The sidewinder moves again. As HONEY watches it and talks, the sidewinder's body slowly inches its way across the stage.

HONEY

Well I don't want to get strangled again. Once is enough. It's moving again! Hey! Hey!

YOUNG MAN

Take it easy. It's all in your mind.

HONEY

It is not in my mind! It's right there! It's moving and rattling and I'm looking right at it! Why don't you look and see for yourself. Please look at it. You're scaring me. I know I'm not going crazy! Who are you anyway! Hey! Talk to me! I've told you everything about me and you haven't told me one thing. Hey!

The YOUNG MAN suddenly grabs her and pulls her to the ground then rolls over on top of her. He kisses her and feels her up. HONEY screams and squirms. Another flash of light from above. The beam of light across the sky. The sidewinder lights up red and twitches wildly. The rattle grows louder as it inches its way across the stage.

HONEY

What are you doing! Let go of me! Let me go! Stop! Stop it! Get off! Get off of me! My husband's going to get you for this! Dukie! Help! Help! Somebody!

The YOUNG MAN rips off her blouse and starts kissing her tits and stomach. HONEY gets turned on and runs her fingers through his hair.

Oh. Oh. OOOOOOOOH. Yes. Yes. Oh. Lick me. Lick me. Yes. Oh. You're fantastic. Oh. Yes. Yes. Yes. Lick me! Lick me!

The YOUNG MAN stops suddenly and stands up, straddling HONEY with his legs.

What's the matter? You can kiss me. It's all right. What's wrong? You're really weird, mister. I'm leaving. I want to leave!

The YOUNG MAN looks up at the sky with his back to the audience and stares. HONEY begins to panic. From this point on there are more frequent blasts of blue light. Each time the sidewinder lights up alternately green and red and the rattling grows louder as he slithers and inches across the stage.

YOUNG MAN

It's all going to happen now.

HONEY

What is? I'm leaving here!

She tries to leave. The YOUNG MAN puts his foot gently on her chest and pushes her back down.

YOUNG MAN

You can't. We're caught. We're captured.

HONEY

Not me! Nobody's capturing me or kidnapping me or anything else! I'm free! I can come and go anywhere I like! You can't make me stay here!

YOUNG MAN

You're right.

He lets her up. She stands but can't move. She seems almost hypnotized.

HONEY

Wait a minute. Wait . . . What did you give me anyway? What was in that needle? You're no diabetic! I've seen diabetics before and you're not one of them! Who are you anyway? How did you get here? Where are you from?

YOUNG MAN

>I am from the planet Crypton. No. I am from the Hollywood Hills. No. I am from Freak City. That's where I was raised anyway. A small town. A town like any other town. A town like Mama used to make with lace doilies and apple pie and incest and graft. No. It's not true. I am an American though. Despite what they say. In spite of the scandal. I am truly an American. I was made in America. Born, bred and raised. I have American scars on my brain. Red, white and blue. I bleed American blood. I dream American dreams. I fuck American girls. I devour the planet. I'm an earth eater. No. I'm a lover of peace. A peace maker. A flower child, burned by the times. Burned out. A speed freak. A Tootsie Roll, an Abazaba. I came to infect the continent. To spread my disease. To make my mark, to make myself known. To cut down the trees, to dig out the gold, to shoot down the deer, to capture the wind. But now I'm myself. Now I'm here. And it's all going to happen now. Right now. It's all going to happen.

>*HONEY collapses.*

BLACKOUT

>*Bright flash of light. Beams of light go back and forth across the sky. Then back to blackness. A sonic boom. Above the proscenium a large neon "Intermission" sign in red blinks on and off continuously as the song "Alien Song" by the HOLY MODAL ROUNDERS comes on.*

OPERATION SIDEWINDER
music by HOLY MODAL ROUNDERS

ALIEN SONG

You don't have to do me no favors
You don't have to tell me no lies
Just tell me what happened to my neighbors
When all I can see is black flies

It wasn't so long that I wandered
It wasn't so long I was gone
But now I come back and there's no wooden shack
And the turnips I grew are all gone

You don't look to me like a native
The way that you move is so strange
I wish I was feeling creative
But maybe it's time for a change

Maybe I took the wrong highway
Maybe I made a mistake
But this is the creek where I caught pollywogs
And I know 'cause I just took a drink

Maybe we could make conversation
I see that your lips have no skin
There must be a simple explanation
But how come you're wearing a grin

I couldn't go back where I came from
'Cause that would just bring me back here
And this is the place I was born, bred and raised
And it doesn't seem like I was ever here

It looks like your forehead's on fire
But maybe I'm losing my grip

It sounds like your voice is a choir
And now both my feet seem to slip

Now I can see my whole body
Stranded way down by the creek
It looks so alone while it looks for its home
And it doesn't hear me while I shriek

by SAM SHEPARD

ACT TWO
OPERATION

SIDEWINDER

MICKEY FREE

SCENE 1

Black stage. The houselights go down. The sun glows on stage and becomes brighter and brighter revealing the '57 Chevy seen in Act one, center stage. The three Blacks are seated inside. They are on the desert. The radio in the car is blaring Booker T. and the M.G.'s "Green Onions." The Blacks sit motionless and listen to the tune for a full sixty seconds. Then BLOOD turns the radio off with a sharp snap. DUDE and BLADE slowly open their doors on either side and get out of the car. They slam the doors shut and walk to the back of the car as BLOOD sits motionless behind the wheel staring straight ahead.

DUDE

Keys, Blood!

BLOOD takes the keys out of the ignition and without looking back, puts his arm out the window and tosses them back to DUDE who catches them. DUDE unlocks the trunk and raises it. Inside are the YOUNG MAN and HONEY with their hands tied behind their backs and gags in their mouths. DUDE and BLADE lift them out of the trunk and pull them around to the downstage side of the car and slam them up against it. The YOUNG MAN and HONEY make muffled screams and protests as DUDE and BLADE pull out guns and level them at their heads, as though to execute the two of them.

BLOOD

Hold it!

BLOOD opens his door and slides out. He walks up to HONEY and the YOUNG MAN and stares at them, then reaches up simultaneously with both hands and grabs their gags and yanks them out of their mouths.

YOUNG MAN
Hey Blood, what's . . . .

BLOOD
Shut up!

HONEY
You guys better not hurt us. They got Forest Rangers out here. They make the rounds every half hour.

YOUNG MAN
What's going on, Blood? Did something go wrong?

BLOOD
Yeah, something went wrong. Your friend Mickey Free didn't make the drop.

YOUNG MAN
What? Why not? What happened?

BLOOD
You tell me.

YOUNG MAN
I left him with the dope. I trusted him completely.

BLOOD
Seems as though he took off into the desert with a very valuable computer and just forgot all about our plan.

YOUNG MAN

I don't know anything about a computer.

BLOOD

It also seems like there's a couple dead men in a garage somewhere who can easily be traced to a Volkswagen which can be easily traced to us.

YOUNG MAN

I had to shoot them. They were slowing me down.

HONEY

You shot somebody? You never told me you shot anybody.

YOUNG MAN

Shut up!

BLOOD

One thing I figured sure was that we could shape a psychedelic head any which way once we gave it the proper injections. Once we set it straight on a few political scores. 'Course there might be such a thing as an overdose of that technique. I mean I can dig it. The revolution looks old fashioned once you seen the universe. Ain't I right now. I mean all them lovelies floatin' around the street lookin' for a taste of acid pants and some insights into their karma and the right sign to match up to theirs. I mean there ain't much of a choice between balling all day and getting high or becoming a responsible revolutionary. Now ain't that the truth. I mean shoot, you didn't spend all them years fightin' the draft just to get the same bullshit from a bunch of crazy Blackmen.

YOUNG MAN
> O.K. man, look.

BLOOD
> Oh, now he's calling me man! He speakin' my language! Yeah, brother! Bring on the chitlins! You gonna have to be a whole lot hipper than hip to get out of this mess, chump.

YOUNG MAN
> I'm trying to talk to you!

BLOOD
> Rap!

YOUNG MAN
> I ran into a jam at a garage. The car was doing weird things. So I went into this garage to get it checked out. I was there for a couple hours trying to get it fixed. Then this crazy guy comes running into the gas station saying his wife got bit by a huge snake or something.

HONEY
> When was that? You never told me about that.

YOUNG MAN
> Just shut up!

HONEY
> That was me he was talking about.

YOUNG MAN
> Shut up! So this guy comes running in and gets the

mechanic all hung up in his thing. So I shot him. I shot them both.

HONEY

That was Dukie! That was my Dukie! You shot him! You shot my Dukie!

HONEY starts screaming and kicking at the YOUNG MAN. BLOOD gives a command and BLADE steps in and jams the gag back in HONEY's mouth. She goes on sobbing and kicking.

BLOOD

(*to young man*) You're real stupid. You know that?

YOUNG MAN

Come on, Blood. I did everything you told me.

BLOOD

But nothing worked! Nothing worked! You fucked up! Now we're right back where we started.

YOUNG MAN

I can find Mickey. I'll go look for him and find out what happened.

BLOOD

There's bigger stakes now.

YOUNG MAN

What do you mean?

BLOOD

The Sidewinder Computer. That snake you heard that guy screaming about?

YOUNG MAN
>What about it?

BLOOD
>We want that snake. We want it bad. You dig?

>*A FOREST RANGER enters from right. The Blacks are very cool. HONEY desperately tries to gesture to the RANGER.*

RANGER
>You folks having trouble?

BLOOD
>Yeah. As a matter of fact we are. We've been trying to get to Ubehebe Crater for the past hour and a half now and we haven't been able to find it.

RANGER
>Well you folks should have stopped in at the Ranger station before venturing off on your own. This desert's no place to play around in.

BLOOD
>Yeah, we realized that but we just got so excited about seeing the sights that we couldn't wait.

RANGER
>Things are especially dangerous now since there were two men killed not too far from here just last week. We still haven't found the killer.

BLOOD
>Is that right. Well if we see anything we'll ....

RANGER
>Is the young lady all right?

BLOOD

Sure, she just got a little sun stroke.

RANGER

What's she got in her mouth?

BLOOD

A wet cloth. They say that's the best thing for a sun stroke.

RANGER

Well not stuffed in her mouth like that. She's liable to suffocate.

BLOOD

She'll be all right in a little while.

RANGER

Say, how come she's tied up like that? Now wait a minute. I'm no fool.

BLOOD pulls out a gun and levels it at the RANGER.

BLOOD

You're the biggest fool around baby. Now drop your gun. Go on!

There is a long pause as the RANGER considers what to do next. Suddenly he tries to draw his gun and BLOOD fires three shots into him. He falls dead. HONEY sobs through her gag. BLOOD points the gun at the YOUNG MAN's head.

BLOOD

Now you got one last chance to redeem yourself Charlie. That extra sized snake that Mickey Free's got is something we need. We need it bad. Now I want you to find it and bring it back to us. The head and all. You dig? Now if you goof once more I suggest that you and your foxey lady here head for south of the border and start yourself a pot farm or something 'cause we're gonna be after your ass.

BLOOD turns the YOUNG MAN around and cuts his arms loose with a knife.

YOUNG MAN

I can travel better on my own. Can't you take her back with you?

BLOOD

She's gonna lead you to that snake boy. Now you cut her loose.

BLOOD hands the knife to the YOUNG MAN.

BLACKOUT

"Bad Karma" is played.

OPERATION SIDEWINDER
music by HOLY MODAL ROUNDERS

BAD KARMA

I got that bad karma baby
Gonna lay it on you
Got that bad karma baby
Nothing better to do
And when that bad karma hits you
Gonna holler and moan
Got that bad karma baby
Gonna bring it all home
I try so hard
I try to behave
But that bad karma baby gonna lead me to my grave.

I'm as down as a wart hog on a summer day
I'm as down as a depth charge in my own sweet way
I'm a down bringing back biting evil thing doer
I was born in an outhouse and I live in a sewer
I try so hard
I try to behave
But that bad karma baby gonna lead me to my grave.

When I'm reincarnated I get meaner yet
You may think I'm the lowest it's a damn good bet
But if I ain't the lowest I'll find out who is
And if his karma's badder I will rip off his
I try so hard
I try to behave
But that bad karma baby gonna lead me to my grave.

by PETER STAMPFEL & ANTONIA

SCENE

The song fades out. Candles are lit on stage. Soft yellow light comes up revealing a small cave in the mountains. The home of the SPIDER LADY. She is a wizened old Indian shaman with long white hair, Mexican blankets hung around her shoulders and across her lap, long tooth and bone necklaces, turquoise rings, etc. She is seated cross-legged in the cave to stage left with several candles around her. Seated directly across from her is MICKEY FREE with the sidewinder's head held in his cupped hands and the red eyes blinking on and off and the tongue spitting out. Behind them, upstage in the cave are the two INDIANS seen with MICKEY FREE in Act One. They are also seated cross-legged and pass a small bowl of steaming liquid back and forth between them from which they drink. Around them are their rifles, ammunition and more candles. Hanging from the roof of the cave are several long ribbons, red fox tails and religious artifacts. Bowls of incense are lit and placed in niches in the wall of the cave with smoke gently rising out of them.

MICKEY FREE

I am afraid, Spider Lady. I find myself holding a great power. I have not the wisdom to use it. Speak to me of its secret.

SPIDER LADY

A great war is about to begin. It will mark the end of the Fourth World and the preparation for the Emergence to the Fifth. Do not be afraid, Mickey Free. You have a part to play in this Emergence. Do not seek shelter. It is only materialistic people who seek to make shelters. Those who are at peace in their own hearts already are in the great shelter of life. There is no shelter for evil. Those who take no part in the making of world division are ready to resume life in another world. They are all one, brothers. The war will be a spiritual conflict with material things. Material matters will be destroyed by spiritual beings who will remain to create one world and one nation under one power, that of the Creator. The time is not far off. The head of this serpent spirit has come to you as a sign. You must see it through to its rightful end.

MICKEY FREE

What does it mean? This spirit head.

SPIDER LADY

In the beginning there were the Star Gods. They descended to earth in flaming discs and created two great clans of man. One, the Snake Clan, the other the Lizard. To each were given tasks. The Lizard Clan was to harvest the crops and raise the children and the Snake Clan was to see to the spiritual needs of the people. For this purpose the Snake Clan was given a giant spirit snake to communicate with the Gods and keep peace in the hearts of the people. The Lizard Clan soon grew jealous and wanted the giant snake for its own. There came a day of the great tug of war between the two clans. The Lizard Clan pulling the head, the Snake Clan pulling the tail. Suddenly the serpent spirit split in two parts, the head going with the Lizard Clan, the tail going with the Snake. At that moment it is said, the people lost all knowledge of their origin. The Gods vanished from the earth. The people were lost.

The two tribes went separate ways and wandered endlessly and with no purpose. More and more people left the clans and wandered their separate ways, taking up homes and founding separate communities, until all over the earth there was mistrust and hatred. Then a vision occurred to a small group of chosen ones who today live on the high mesas of this desert. A blue star descended to earth in the form of a spirit from the Star Gods and told the people that their Emergence was at hand. It spoke of the severed halves of the ancient spirit snake and that they soon would be joined together again on a night of the great dance. That once the two halves were joined the people would be swept from the earth by a star, for they were to be saved from the destruction at hand. That soon after the spirit snake would again be pulled in half by the evil ones and the Fourth World would come to an end.

MICKEY FREE

What must I do?

SPIDER LADY

You must be strong. For too long now you have been used by the white man's cavalry, Mickey Free. You have cheated your red brothers to the south. You have tracked and hunted down your own kind for the white man's money. . . .

MICKEY FREE

And for my freedom! Better to hunt and kill than to be trapped behind bars in their camp! How could I choose! Geronimo was ready to surrender! I had no choice!

SPIDER LADY

> You must let this head speak to your heart, Mickey Free. You must see the truth of this myth I have told you. You can read it in the earth itself. In the stars. Within your own conscience. Take this powerful spirit and deliver it to those who await it. To the Chosen Ones atop the high mesa.

MICKEY FREE

> But what of the body? I have lost the body.

SPIDER LADY

> It will come. It is written. All things have a plan, Mickey Free.

> *MICKEY FREE bows his head slowly to the SPIDER LADY as the lights dim out.*

> *"I Disremember Quite Well" is played.*

OPERATION SIDEWINDER
music by HOLY MODAL ROUNDERS

I DISREMEMBER QUITE WELL

You'll pardon me if I act strange
but we've been out of touch
I know that time is on your side
but time can do so much.
Are you still making it with time?
I disremember quite well

Yes I can see as I come close
time has been good to you
Just for a moment's truth you almost
had the face I knew.
But now, of course, it's not for real
I disremember quite well

I used to know you when you turned
your water into wine.
You played the shell game with yourself
and won it every time.
But where are you going to keep your prize?
I disremember quite well

I used to walk on water too
and float above the sand.
And hang the stars like diamonds on my
outstretched greedy hands.
But I've forgotten how that game goes
I disremember quite well

And did you ever do whatever thing
it is you're for?

Or does an old idea like that have meaning
anymore?
The maybe that I loved has gone, but where?
I disremember quite well

by ANTONIA

SCENE 3

The song fades out. A woman STENOGRAPHER's VOICE is heard in the dark.

STENOGRAPHER'S VOICE
Ready, Captain Bovine!

CAPTAIN BOVINE'S VOICE
All right. Let's see 'em.

A large color slide is shown on the upstage wall in the darkness. All the slides are of outlaws from the 1800's. CAPTAIN BOVINE speaks in the dark. The slides keep changing.

CAPTAIN BOVINE'S VOICE
Now these faces that you're gonna see here, Billy, are all known criminals that, as yet, we haven't been able to pin down. Besides the young man in question here, if you happen to run across any other faces that you might have seen on the desert, it would be more than helpful if you pointed them out.

BILLY'S VOICE
Nope. Not a one.

BOVINE'S VOICE
Well, take your time now. We got a whole stack to go through.

The faces keep flashing on the wall upstage. They get faster and faster as they go on, creating a strobe effect.

91

Any identifying marks that you can remember? I mean besides the long hair and bare feet. That's pretty common amongst your outlaws anyhow. Any scars or things like that?

BILLY'S VOICE

Nope. Nary a one.

BOVINE'S VOICE

Did he have an accent? A limp? Anything at all would be helpful, Billy.

BILLY'S VOICE

Nope. Healthy as a yearling colt, that one.

BOVINE'S VOICE

What about the others? Any of the others ring a bell?

BILLY'S VOICE

Nope. Nary a one.

The last slide is a full head shot of the YOUNG MAN with a moustache. It stops still.

BOVINE'S VOICE

Shall we go through 'em once more for you, Billy? You might have missed a couple and it's very important for our records.

BILLY'S VOICE

I think not. I mean—— I think——

BOVINE'S VOICE

Yes?

BILLY'S VOICE

You folks wouldn't have a hot cup a' java layin' around the back room here, would ya'? Jest a little somethin' to wet the old whistle.

DR. VECTOR'S VOICE

Java? Java.

GENERAL'S VOICE

Lights please, Edith!

The lights pop up revealing BILLY with his pots and pans sitting in a chair downstage with his back to the audience and his pack on the floor beside him. Next to him is the STENOGRAPHER, Edith, who is shutting off the projector and turning the lights on, etc. GENERAL BROWSER and COLONEL WARNER are sitting behind a table upstage, facing BILLY. CAPTAIN BOVINE, Chief Inspector for the CIA, paces around the middle of the stage, chain smoking cigarettes and dressed in a gray suit. DOCTOR VECTOR is also seated at the table with the COLONEL and GEN-ERAL BROWSER.

GENERAL

Edith, would you get Billy a cup of coffee, please. Do you take cream and sugar, Billy?

BILLY

Nope. Black like midnight.

The STENOGRAPHER goes out and closes the door. The room is plastered with Air Force insignia, the flag, photographs of planes, the desert, slogans, etc., including: "To protect and to serve" in large letters. The three pistols that the YOUNG MAN gave to BILLY are sitting on the desk in front of the GENERAL. CAPTAIN BOVINE walks up to them.

CAPTAIN BOVINE

Now, Billy, you're gonna have to understand something here right off the bat. Unless we come up with some evidence leading us to this kid you say you got these guns off of then we got no other choice than to assume that these weapons belong to you.

BILLY

Oh now don't go handin' me that malarkey, Captain Bovine. What the hell's a prospector out in the middle a' no man's land gonna do with three new-fangled irons like them.

CAPTAIN BOVINE

Exactly. What is he going to do?

BILLY

Nothin'! He's gonna hand 'em over to Mickey Free like he said he was 'cause Danny paid him to. That's what. Nothin' else. Shucks, the way you fellas carry on here anyone'd think there's a plot goin' on to overturn the damn government.

CAPTAIN BOVINE

Danny? Did you say Danny? Was that the kid's name? Answer me, Billy! There's no point covering up for him. If we don't get him someone else will.

BILLY

Danny, Johnny, Jimmy! I don't know what his handle was. I never paid it no never mind. We just got to know each other so well we didn't need no names.

BOVINE

Now listen, Billy. You may not realize it, since you've

been out of touch with society for some time, but this country's in trouble. Big trouble. Over the past few years there's been a general breakdown of law and order and a complete disrespect for the things we've held sacred since our ancestors founded this country. This country needs you, Billy. It needs your help to help root out these subversive, underground creeps and wipe the slate clean once and for all. You don't realize the trouble they've been giving us. Every time there's a holiday or a bunch of people want to have a good time and just peacefully cele- brate some national hero or something, there's al- ways a bunch of these creeps hanging around mak- ing faces and giving the finger and shouting ob- scene things around and carrying cards and doing wild dances and what not. It's become worse than a disgrace, Billy. It's not even funny anymore. There was a time when the whole thing was a joke. But not anymore. Now they've got sympathizers, inside agitators and con-men in the White House. All over the country it's going on. I saw it all coming a long time ago. Ever since those bushy haired creeps started infiltrating from England in 1964. Before that even. Playing Negro music and gyrating their bodies and stuff like that. I'm telling you, Billy, it's about time we brought this whole thing to an end. If we don't do something soon we'll be overrun with these creepy faggots and leather jacket types. Things have stayed the same for too long now. It's time for a change!

The STENOGRAPHER enters with the coffee and gives it to BILLY. Then she sits down behind a steno machine and starts taking down the proceedings as though it were a court trial.

STENOGRAPHER
Here you are, Billy. A nice hot cup of java.

DR. VECTOR
Java?

BILLY
Well now. That's fine. Thank ya', peaches.

STENOGRAPHER
You're welcome.

GENERAL
Captain Bovine, perhaps we could find out something more about this Mickey Free.

CAPTAIN BOVINE
Later. First I want to nail this kid. He's the source.
Mickey Free was obviously a go between, just like
Billy here. How does that make you feel, Billy? To
know that you were used by this punk.

BILLY
No different. I knew it all along. Me and him was
pals. I coulda' cared less about what his real aims
were. We just struck it off real fine and let me tell
ya', that's a rarity on the desert. Yessir. Why I could
tell you stories——

CAPTAIN BOVINE
Good. Tell us a story right now, Billy. The story of
how you met this kid and everything you can remember about him. We'll listen.

BILLY

Well I was out near the Harmony Borax Works out there trying to tap a vein that I'd had me an eye on for quite a spell. Seems like forever. Well, with me ya' know, it's more of a way a' life than anything else. I mean not like them weekenders what come out fer a taste a yeller fever, all hog tied with them electric Geiger counters and metallic metal finders and what all. Us old timers, a lot of us, don't really hanker for no heavy pay loads. Naw. Just a little chicken scratch to keep the vittles comin' is cause enough to keep us on.

CAPTAIN BOVINE

What about this kid?

BILLY

I'm a gettin' there, mister. And don't get yer hackles up on this old buzzard, sonny, 'cause I'm as likely to clam up on ya' as spew on about somethin' close to my heart when I ain't got no willin' ears to catch it.

CAPTAIN BOVINE

All right. I'm sorry.

BILLY

I come down off the shale part a' the slope and headed toward my burro when I look and see this here kid what appears to be takin' a sun bath. Yeah. Right out in the middle of the blazin' sun he's a lyin' on his backside and gazin' right into thet big yeller ball. So I walks up and right off I offer him some rashers and a hot cup a' java. Figured he could use somethin' in that belly. Looked like it ain't done

nothin' but gurgle for the last fifty miles. So we set
ourselves down and get right into talkin' and spin-
nin' yarns. And let me tell ya' he had some doozers.

CAPTAIN BOVINE

What did you talk about?

BILLY

Well, he told me some a' the galldarndest tales I
ever did hear. Dope peddlers, prostitutes, pretty girls
and I don't know what all. Told me one about some
street up in Frisco where he stayed and had hisself
a different woman every darn night for over a week.
Now don't that beat all? Enough to make an old man
skiddadle off the desert like a water bug.

CAPTAIN BOVINE

Did he ask you any questions?

BILLY

Danny? Never seen nobody with so many questions.
Day in and day out he'd be askin' me stuff about
the desert, the Indians, the sky, the night, the sun,
the stars, any damn thing he could lay his brain on.

CAPTAIN BOVINE

How much time did he spend with you then?

BILLY

Must a' been well over a fortnight.

CAPTAIN BOVINE

How long is that? Let me see. A fortnight?

BILLY

> Better part of a couple weeks. I thought you coppers was supposed to know everything.

CAPTAIN BOVINE

> All right. It slipped my mind. You say he asked you about the Indians. What did he ask?

BILLY

> Everything. Their magic, how they cooked corn. Where the reservations were. How to get to them. The different drugs and medicine. How to tell the tribes. The symbols, the legends, the religion. How to make water out of sand. Stuff like that. So after a while I figured if he was so all het up about the red man I might as well introduce him to a real live one. Let him learn from the horse's mouth. So I took him up to meet Mickey Free. He ain't a full blood but a half breed has all the wits of a Indian plus the gumption of a white man. Mickey's one a the few real wild ones left. I believe you boys might a' even heard tell of him. Seems like he helped ya' find yer-selves some a' this Indian land yer settin' on right now.

GENERAL

> Yes. The name rings a bell.

BILLY

> Yup. Old Mick's been doin' dirty work for white men ever since he was knee high to a scorpion. Most Injuns hate his guts. Say he's cold-blooded, turns in his own kind. Yup. He's the one supposed to have

out-foxed Geronimo. Boxed him into a canyon or
somethin'.

COLONEL

Captain Bovine, do we have to sit here all day listen-
ing to this? There's important business at hand!

GENERAL

Please, Warner.

CAPTAIN BOVINE

Let me handle this, gentlemen. Now listen, Billy.
You'll have to understand that what we're primarily
interested in here is the young man who gave you
these guns and how it's tied up with these Indian
affairs. You can skip all the local color.

BILLY

Well I'll try to scrape it right down to the bone for
you fellas, but there's an awful lot bouncin' around
this old head a' mine. Can't rightly figure where one
thing leaves off and the other begins.

CAPTAIN BOVINE

We understand. It would help if you could clear up
the connection between Mickey Free and this punk
for us.

BILLY

Well, like I say. I left Johnny off up there at Mickey's
wikiup. They hit it off like grease hits the skillet,
them two. Just a cracklin' back and forth between
'em. They stuck it out together for quite a spell, then
that blond boy up and left. He come back to me and
started talkin' all different from what he done be-

fore. Talkin' about a plan with a bunch a poor folk back in the city. How I was to figure in this plan by deliverin' guns to Mickey. Then one night I'm sittin' out there in a lonely spot, moonlit and all, waitin' for Danny when I hears these low kind a' moanin' sounds and I looks down and layin' right in front a' me there is——

CAPTAIN BOVINE
Just the pertinent facts, Billy!

BILLY
Boy, I do believe you fellas wouldn't let the light a' day shine on a sidewinder in the zoo, 'less you had the keeper there beside ya'.

DR. VECTOR stands abruptly.

DR. VECTOR
Sidewinder! Did what you say was sidewinder?

GENERAL
Take it easy, Doc. Sit down.

COLONEL
He did say "sidewinder" though. I heard him say it.

CAPTAIN BOVINE
Why did you mention the word "sidewinder," Billy?

BILLY
Just came off the top of the head, gents. The Hopis say the top of the head has a door and if you keep that door open all kind a' wonders come to ya'.

CAPTAIN BOVINE

Have you ever heard that word used on the desert before?

BILLY

You must be pullin' my long johns, sonny. That's a snake. A tiny poisonous rattler what likes the shade and——

CAPTAIN BOVINE

Did you ever hear the kid use that word? Answer me!

BILLY

I think if it's all the same to you, boys, I'll just mosey on.

BILLY starts to get up. CAPTAIN BOVINE shoves him back down in his seat. DR. VECTOR sits back down.

CAPTAIN BOVINE

You'll stay right here until you're released. Withholding information from a government official is punishable by law, in case you're not aware of it.

BILLY

Well slap my daddy. Thought I was too old to get myself into more trouble.

CAPTAIN BOVINE

Whether you like it or not, Billy, you've gotten yourself mixed up in a pretty messy situation. A very confidential government authorized computer has escaped from this Air Force base. This computer goes under the code name of "Sidewinder." Your mention of the name has only further confirmed our suspicions that you are in some way connected with its disappearance. Unless you reveal to us more useful information in this regard then I will have no other recourse than to arrest you for possession of arms without a license.

BILLY

The only reason I was— It was just a figure o' speech. I mean—I was a' gettin' set to tell ya' about this other snake that I seen.

DR. VECTOR rises again. The GENERAL coaxes him back in his wheelchair.

DR. VECTOR

Snake! What snake?

BILLY

Like I say, I was waitin' for my rendezvous with Danny when I hears these groanin' sounds comin' out a' the night. I looks down and there in front of me I sees this pretty young thing all tangled up in the biggest most gigantic galldanged sidewinder I ever did see. I mean I think it was a sidewinder. It had them tell-tale horns over the eye sockets. But she was so damn big!

DR. VECTOR lets out a jubilant shout. He starts buzzing around in his wheelchair.

DR. VECTOR

That's it! My sidewinder! It's alive! My sidewinder is alive! It lives! It lives! It lives! My beautiful side-winder lives! Beautiful, beautiful sidewinder!

GENERAL
Doctor, please! Dr. Vector! Calm yourself!

BILLY
Nope. It's dead.

DR. VECTOR's wheelchair comes to a screeching halt.

DR. VECTOR
Dead!

BILLY
I mean I think so. It has to be.

DR. VECTOR
What does this mean! You just said it lived! It was alive!

COLONEL
What's this all about.

CAPTAIN BOVINE
Explain yourself, Billy.

BILLY
Well I seen the head up on top of the high mesa with Mickey. They were worshipping the damn thing. Minus the body. I went lookin' for Mickey up at his wikiup but he'd flew the coop. Couple a' his side kicks says he went off to the high mesa to take part in some ritual of the tribes. So I followed his trail and sure enough there he was right in the middle a' the most high falootin' ceremony I ever did see. And I seen plenty. Lots a' tribes were there. All gathered together peaceable like and gathered around the snake head like it were some kind a' god or somethin'. And there

was Mickey, old "one eye" himself, just a' sittin' there pretty as ya' please, beamin' from ear to ear and holdin' that head right in his lap. So I sallies over to him and show him the guns. Figured he'd be pleased as punch. But nothin' doin'. All of a sudden the whole shootin' match comes to a dead stop and they all just stand there a' starin' right at me like I brought the devil his self. Well right off the bat I could tell I done somethin' out a' step. Then I look in Mickey's face and see that toothy grin a' his disappear fast as a swaller and he stands up and looks real serious and sad and mad all at once and tells me he don't want nothin' never more to do with guns or killin'. I mean I like to drop my silver fillin's right on the spot. Words like that comin' from the most feared Injun killin' bronco the West ever knowed. Then he reaches in his pouch and pulls out these here little plastic bags and tells me to take the guns and these bags back to the white devil what he got 'em from.

CAPTAIN BOVINE

What bags? What do you mean?

BILLY

Right here. I got 'em right in my pack.

BILLY reaches into his pack and pulls out the plastic bags of dope that the YOUNG MAN had given MICKEY FREE in Act One. BOVINE snatches them away. Rips them open, wets his finger and sticks it in the bag, then tastes the powder. He marches to the telephone and picks it up.

CAPTAIN BOVINE

Hello. Get me a special detail of Desert Tactical Troops over here immediately. It's an emergency!

BOVINE hangs up the phone. BILLY stands.

DR. VECTOR
But what of my sidewinder!

BILLY
You can't send no soldiers out there, Captain Bovine. They'll interfere with the ceremony. The Indians won't hanker to it one bit. You better pick up that phone and call off them troops. I ain't kiddin', Captain. That's serious business them red skins are up to. I wouldn't mess with it to save my soul.

CAPTAIN BOVINE
Pipe down, old timer. It's just a routine checkup.

BLACKOUT

"CIA Man" comes on in the dark.

OPERATION SIDEWINDER
music by HOLY MODAL ROUNDERS

C.I.A. MAN

Who can tell if Egypt's got the bomb
Even if the atmosphere is calm

Fuckin A Man C.I.A. Man

Who can train guerillas by the dozen
Train 'em all to kill their untrained cousins

Fuckin A Man C.I.A. Man

Who can plant the bug on anyone
Who would never eavesdrop just for fun

Fuckin A Man C.I.A. Man

Who will do just what he has to do
All the way from Dallas to Peru

Fuckin A Man C.I.A. Man

Why is Mao scared to start a hassle
Mao isn't man enough to rassle

Fuckin A Man C.I.A. Man

Who is diplomatically immune
Who else but the hero of this tune

Fuckin A Man C.I.A. Man

by PETER STAMPEL, TULI KUPFERBURG
& ANTONIA

SCENE 4

The song fades out. Total silence. Black stage. Thundering sound of many feet pounding on the floor. Silence. Low moaning sound of many voices chanting in unison.

HOPI CHANTS

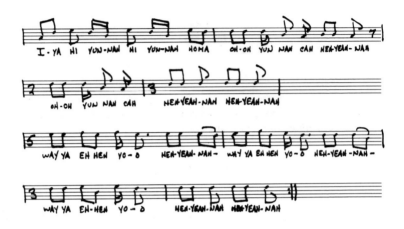

The lights come up slowly as the chanting goes on. Center
stage is MICKEY FREE's wikiup, a small oval shaped struc-
ture made out of bent twigs, old sheets of metal, mud,
strips of cloth and a dark blanket covering the door. A thin
column of smoke comes from the top. Stage left of the
wikiup is a group of eight INDIANS seated in a semi-circle
around an open pit. These are the SNAKE PRIESTS. They
are chanting and preparing themselves for a ceremony. In
front of them are three large pottery jars, the tops covered
with antelope skins. Behind them is the snake altar: a large
screen of antelope skin stetched on four long sticks. Three
large Hopi Kachina dolls are painted on the skin with other
symbols, semi-circles and figures. Large snake bodies and
heads protrude from the skin in bright colors; these operate like hand puppets from behind the screen, so at a
certain point in the ceremony they will come alive and
wriggle to the dance.

In front of the screen are several stalks of corn and tall

poles with feather and ribbon streamers dangling from
their tops. Encircling the entire group and the altar is a
line of sacred yellow cornmeal. All the INDIANS are very
dark skinned, have long black hair with eagle feathers at
the back of the neck, are naked except for loin cloths and
moccasins. A large white oval is painted over each of their
breasts and shoulder blades, their foreheads and the fronts
of their throats are painted white, the rest of their faces
are painted black, the forearms and legs below the knees
are painted white. They each wear turquoise and shell
necklaces; their loin cloths are blue with a black snake
design in front and back. They wear belts with long fringe
around the waist, and a fox skin and tail fastened to the
belt in the rear. Tied to each right knee is a tortoise shell
rattle. Their moccasins are reddish brown buckskin with
fringe and shell designs. They wear white armlets around
the bicep and anklets just above the moccasins. The CHIEF
SNAKE PRIEST, who sits more or less in the center, holds
a bow standard decorated with feathers and horsehair.

They chant in a low moaning unison for a while and sway
from side to side. The CHIEF SNAKE PRIEST slowly places
both his hands on one of the jars, the others follow and
place their hands on the other two jars. The CHIEF re-
moves the skin from the top of the jar and tips the jar
toward the pit. The other priests do the same with their
jars. The chanting mounts in volume and intensity. Sud-

*denly, on cue from the CHIEF, they all dip the jars down
into the pit. Dozens of snakes of all sizes and colors slither
from the jars into the pit. The chanting keeps up until all
the snakes have disappeared into the pit.*

*HONEY and the YOUNG MAN pop onto the stage from
left; the sidewinder's body is in the YOUNG MAN's hand.
The INDIANS are jolted into silence. The YOUNG MAN and
HONEY stare at them. The INDIANS rise in unison and
walk off left.*

HONEY
Maybe we oughta' come back tomorrow.

YOUNG MAN
Shut up.

HONEY
Look, I've done my bit already. I found you your
dumb snake so why don't you let me go. You said
before that I just slowed you down.

YOUNG MAN
I need you around.

HONEY
'Cause you're scared. You've been scared right along
and you thought I didn't know it. Right? You're
scared shitless.

YOUNG MAN
Will you cool it!

HONEY
No, I won't cool it! I'm not one of your hippie sluts

you can drag through the streets and any damn place you feel like going! Giving her clap and hepatitis and everything else.

YOUNG MAN

Look——

HONEY

No, you look! You killed my Dukie! I'll never forgive you for that. Just 'cause I go to bed with you doesn't mean I forgot.

YOUNG MAN

Just hang loose a little bit longer, all right? Please? I promise as soon as we're through getting this snake put back together we'll go into town and have a really neat time. O.K.?

HONEY

Can we go to the movies?

YOUNG MAN

Sure. Anything you want. We'll get us some hot apple pie and coffee at the truck stop and then we'll go to the movies.

HONEY

There's a new Elvis Presley movie on. Did you see it?

The low sound of chanting comes from the wikiup. The YOUNG MAN sneaks toward it with HONEY behind him.

YOUNG MAN

I saw *Jailhouse Rock.*

HONEY

No. This is a new one. He plays the part of this stock car driver who always wins, so he gets real rich. But he's such a good guy that he gives all his money away to his friends and people who are poor. You know, he buys them cars and refrigerators and stoves and TV's and all that kind of stuff. But then he gets in trouble—I mean all his friends like him and everything and he's real popular but he gets in trouble with the Internal Revenue Service because they say he didn't pay a lot of his taxes. So he tells them he wrote off all those gifts as tax deductible charities. But the Internal Revenue doesn't go for that and they say he has to go and take back all those things that he bought for all those people and give them to the government. So he goes and takes back a few things but what happens is that all his friends start hating him because they think he's an Indian giver and everything. So——

Suddenly the two INDIANS who were with MICKEY FREE in Act One jump out of the wikiup with knives and pin the YOUNG MAN and HONEY to the ground. HONEY screams.

YOUNG MAN

Wait a minute! Wait a minute! Paza! Paza! Tanta muy bien amigo! Amigo! Tosa entra por Mickey Free! Nada mas! Nada mas. Para Mickey Free. Entiende? Sabe?

MICKEY FREE comes out of the wikiup slowly. His face is painted with white zigzags. He is stripped to the waist and wears an embroidered loin cloth and high buckskin moccasins and an Apache headband around his head. The huge knife still dangles down from his crotch. He crosses slowly to the YOUNG MAN who is still pinned to the ground. He smiles and releases the INDIANS. They back off.

YOUNG MAN
Mickey.

MICKEY
Kachada. Why have you come back?

YOUNG MAN
I have to talk to you.

MICKEY
I talk no more of guns and drugs. Of plans to conquer worlds. If you come to get back your guns I have already give them to Billy.

YOUNG MAN
No. The guns don't matter. It's the snake. The snake you found on Honey. What did you do with the head?

HONEY
Remember? You saved my life. You cut off its head.

YOUNG MAN
This is the body. You have the head.

The YOUNG MAN holds up the sidewinder's body to MICKEY, who stares at it, then smiles broadly and lets out a shrill scream. He hugs the YOUNG MAN and picks him up, dancing with him and laughing. The other INDIANS smile.

MICKEY
You are the Pahana! You have come! You have brought us our salvation!

MICKEY grabs the sidewinder's body and holds it over his head, dancing with it wildly. The other two INDIANS join in. The YOUNG MAN tries to grab the snake back. HONEY lies dazed on the floor.

YOUNG MAN

Wait a minute! Wait a minute! That's mine! That belongs to somebody else! Mickey! Cut it out! You can't have that snake! They'll kill me if I don't bring it back! Mickey! You've got to give it back! Give it back!

MICKEY

The Spider Lady has told me the truth. She said you would come. The body would join the head of its own will. And now it is here. The ceremony can begin!

YOUNG MAN

What ceremony? That's a machine, you creep! It's not real. The Air Force cooked it up to trace flying saucers! The spades want it to trace the Air Force. I want it because it means my life if I don't get it back to them.

MICKEY

My brothers and I have followed many separate ways, sometimes killing each other. Tonight we shall all see the kingdom. Tonight the spirit snake shall become one again and with it shall join all its people. You and your bride might also come on this journey, Pahana.

HONEY

He's not my husband. He killed my husband.

YOUNG MAN

That's a machine, Mickey. A computer. Not a god.

MICKEY

You are free, Pahana. You have brought us to our Emergence. It will take us to a place we will never come back from. You are welcome to enter and follow us there or stay here on this earth and follow your will. The stars will watch you as you go.

MICKEY turns and walks back into the wikiup with the side-winder's body in his hand. The INDIANS follow him in.

YOUNG MAN

Let's go. Come on.

HONEY

Wait. What did he mean?

YOUNG MAN

Never mind. Let's get out of here.

The chanting comes again from the wikiup, low and then rising.

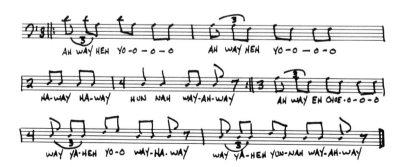

HONEY

What's that?

YOUNG MAN

Never mind! Are you coming or not?

HONEY

I never heard that before.

YOUNG MAN

They're sacred songs. It'd take you a year to understand the first word.

HONEY

It's so soothing. Like hearing the wind.

YOUNG MAN

I know. I know. If you get hooked on it we'll never
get out of here. Now come on! Look, we gotta head
for Mexico right now! Blood is going to be after my
ass before too long. It was you who wanted to go
see the movie before! Remember? Honey! Get up,
and let's go!

*She is in a kind of trance state. She rises slowly and moves
toward the wikiup. The YOUNG MAN runs to her and grabs
her shoulders. He shakes her. She stares at him blankly.*

YOUNG MAN

Goddammit! I'm not walking back down into that
desert alone! Do you hear me! It's the middle of the
night! I might get shot for having long hair or smell-
ing bad or something! Honey! Snap out of it! It's
not for white people's ears! It's secret stuff! It'll
make you crazy! If we go in there they'll never see

us again! Never! We'll be scooped up! Taken away!
Can't you understand me! I need you! I need you
with me! I can't come back here again! Why don't
you listen! Honey!

He shakes her, then lets her go. She walks like a sleep-
walker straight into the wikiup. The chanting reaches a
kind of chord as she enters.

Honey! You'll never see daylight again!

A blue flash in the sky. The sound of a jet as the YOUNG
MAN looks up at the sky. The chanting grows louder. The
YOUNG MAN clenches his hands together and starts to say
the Lord's Prayer as he walks slowly toward the wikiup.

Our Father who art in Heaven. Hallowed be thy name.
Thy kingdom come, thy will be done, on earth as it
is in heaven. Give us this day our daily bread and
forgive us our trespasses as we forgive those who
trespass against us. Lead us not into temptation but
deliver us from evil. For thine is the kingdom, the
power and the glory. Forever and ever. Amen.

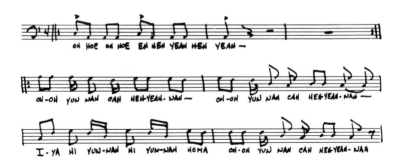

The chanting grows to an incredible pitch as he enters the
wikiup on the word "Amen." A pause as just the wikiup is
seen with the chanting coming from it. Another flash of
blue in the sky. Then the beam of light going across from
stage left to stage right as in Act One. Then one at a time
eight ANTELOPE PRIESTS come out of the wikiup in single
file. They are dressed similarly to the SNAKE PRIESTS except they have painted themselves ash gray with white zigzag lines running up from their breasts to their shoulders,
and down the arms to the fingers and down the front of the
legs to their big toes. They each carry a large gourd-like rattle and one holds a large antelope drum which he pounds in
a steady rhythm. Their chins are outlined by a white line
drawn from ear to ear. Their loin cloths are white with
black snake designs and embroidered sashes. They are
followed closely by the eight SNAKE PRIESTS. They all
continue the chant in a low murmur and walk single file to
the snake altar where they face each other in a double line,
eight on either side of the snake pit. Simultaneously they
stomp with their right feet on the floor. A loud boom like
thunder comes forth. They all begin to sway from left to
right in unison and shake the rattles in time. They form a
circle, then fan out into single file again and circle the
entire stage four times chanting over and over again in
rhythmic pattern and stomping their right feet in unison on
the beginning accent of the word. Each time they stomp,

the sound should come like thunder. The rhythm is slow, deliberate and powerful. Everything about the dance is spiritual and sincere and should not be cartooned or chore-ographed beyond the unison of the rhythmic patterns.

After they have circled the stage four times they again go to the snake pit and line up across from each other, but closer to each other this time and forming a circle of bodies. They link arms and bend over the pit. They make a chord with their voices, rising from a low pitch to ex-tremely high and shrieking. As they do this, the CHIEF PRIEST of the snake group kneels down and puts his head into the pit. He comes up with a snake in his mouth. The others fan back and the CHIEF SNAKE PRIEST dances with the writhing snake in his mouth. The ANTELOPE PRIESTS fan off and dance to the right side of the stage and stand in a line, swaying from side to side and chant-ing as they stomp their right feet.

The SNAKE PRIESTS line up stage left and do the same. One of the SNAKE PRIESTS dances out from the line toward the CHIEF and waves two long eagle feathers over the snake's head as the CHIEF dances with it. The snake goes limp and the CHIEF lets it drop to the floor. A third SNAKE PRIEST dances out with a stick and waves it over the snake then bends down, picks it up with both hands, holds it aloft and dances over to the ANTELOPE PRIESTS. He hands it to one of the ANTELOPE PRIESTS at the end of the line. He takes it and holds it, coaxing it with one hand as he continues to chant. The CHIEF walks back to behind the snake altar where he starts to operate one of the snake puppets in short jerky movements. Another SNAKE PRIEST puts his head into the pit and comes up with another snake between his teeth. The same process goes on as with the CHIEF until each ANTELOPE PRIEST in the line has a snake in his hand and each SNAKE PRIEST has danced with a snake and returned to behind the snake altar to operate one of the puppets. Once this is finished the ANTELOPE PRIESTS are all visible, dancing and chanting with the snakes. The SNAKE PRIESTS are all unseen behind the snake altar, and the snake puppets are moving vigorously around. MICKEY FREE comes out of the wikiup. He is dressed the same way, stripped to the waist, but he wears a blue kachina mask on his head. He holds the head of the sidewinder in his left hand, the body in the right. He holds them aloft. Behind him are HONEY, the YOUNG MAN, and the two INDIANS from before. HONEY's face is painted like the SNAKE PRIESTS' and the YOUNG MAN's like the ANTELOPES'.

HONEY wears a long black dress, a blue loin cloth over it and a white and red cape. Her hair is loose, with eagle feathers attached at the back. Around her neck is a necklace of turquoise and shell. She holds an earthen jar out in front of her containing sacred oil. The YOUNG MAN has an eagle feather tied to the front of his hair, his body is painted ash gray with white zigzag lines like the ANTELOPE PRIESTS' on his body, arms and legs. He also holds a jar filled with oil. The SNAKE PRIESTS come out from behind the altar single file and line up downstage. The ANTELOPES follow suit on the stage right side. One of MICKEY's INDIAN friends leads HONEY by the arm to the line of SNAKE PRIESTS where she kneels in front of the CHIEF.

The YOUNG MAN is led to the ANTELOPES by the other INDIAN and he kneels to their CHIEF PRIEST. Both HONEY and the YOUNG MAN seem to be in a totally different frame of mind now. Calm, spiritual, totally accepting of the whole ritual. MICKEY stands downstage center, changing and holding the segmented sidewinder aloft, moving the two parts toward each other, then away. The SNAKE CHIEF and the ANTELOPE CHIEF exchange places and walk to opposite sides of the stage. The ANTELOPE CHIEF faces HONEY and the SNAKE CHIEF faces the YOUNG MAN. They each simultaneously place their hands

on HONEY's and the YOUNG MAN's heads, then slowly
push their heads down into the jars of oil they hold in
front of them, so that their hair becomes saturated. They
raise their heads up. HONEY and the YOUNG MAN stand.
They are led by the respective CHIEFS downstage in front
of MICKEY FREE. The CHIEF PRIESTS exchange positions
again and then wash HONEY's and the YOUNG MAN's hair
in the oil. They touch their heads together and then twist
their hair together so that it becomes tied. The chanting
continues the whole time.

MICKEY, at the moment HONEY's and the YOUNG MAN's
hair has been tied together, joins the sidewinder's body
to its head. A tremendous bolt of blue light issues from
the sidewinder, matched by one in the sky. Thunder booms.
The sky lights up blue again. The combination of the voices
chanting reaches an incredible shrieking, like lightning. The
whole scene crackles like high voltage wires. Then suddenly everything stops abruptly as three "DESERT TAC-
TICAL TROOPS" with machine guns, pistols, helmets, uni-
forms, etc., enter briskly from right. The INDIANS freeze.

1ST DESERT TACTICAL TROOP
All right! Everybody put up your hands! Everyone!
Put 'em up!

2ND DESERT TACTICAL TROOP
Let's see some identification! That goes for everybody! Get it out!

3RD DESERT TACTICAL TROOP
You people are in big trouble! You got any idea what
you got in your hand there, buddy? That's government property! United States Government property,
buster! Now let's have it!

The 3rd DESERT TACTICAL TROOP grabs for the side-winder which MICKEY still holds over his head. A bright blue light comes from the sidewinder, then from the sky. The D.T.T.'s jump back. All the INDIANS and HONEY and the YOUNG MAN stay frozen.

3RD DESERT TACTICAL TROOP

Now look, buddy! I don't know what's going on here but that snake belongs to us! Now hand it over!

The 3rd DESERT TACTICAL TROOP makes another move toward the sidewinder and again it lights up, answered by a light in the sky.

You wanna get run in for resisting arrest too? We're not playing games here with you punks!

Suddenly MICKEY begins the chant "Wunti Hayano Di-witia" and all the INDIANS plus the YOUNG MAN and HONEY join in. They start to move slowly toward the three DESERT TACTICAL TROOPS with MICKEY leading them, still holding the sidewinder over his head. They begin to form a large circle around the D.T.T.'s as they try to get away from them.

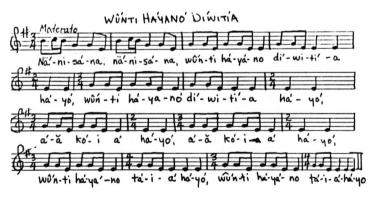

2ND DESERT TACTICAL TROOP
All right! Hold it right there! Hold it!

1ST DESERT TACTICAL TROOP
Stop that singing! Stop where you are!

3RD DESERT TACTICAL TROOP
We're going to open fire in about three seconds if you don't stop and hand over that snake! One! We're not kidding around! Two! This is no joke! We mean business! This is your last chance! Stop in the name of the law! Three!

The DESERT TACTICAL TROOPS open fire on the INDIANS with their machine guns. The INDIANS keep coming. They form a circle with MICKEY at the head of it and the DES- ERT TACTICAL TROOPS in the center firing again and again. The INDIANS just sway back and forth to the rhythm of the chant. The sidewinder lights up, the sky lights up. The 3rd DESERT TACTICAL TROOP rushes straight toward MICKEY FREE, firing his machine gun into him. MICKEY just chants and sways. The 3rd DESERT TACTICAL TROOP reaches up and grabs the sidewinder and yanks it from MICKEY's hands. The body separates from the head again. Bright bolt of blue light from the sky. The D.T.T.'s scream as though being blinded.

The lights go to black after the blue light, then back to bright blue. Each interval of light and dark lasts about five or six seconds. From pitch black to bright blue. Huge gusts of wind blow from upstage directly out into the audience, changing from hot to cold. Wind also blows across stage. Streams of smoke come from all around the proscenium arch and upstage. The chanting increases. A high fre- quency whine. The chanting becomes amplified. The bright blue light flashes on, the INDIANS are in ecstasy as they chant. The D.T.T.'s are cringing on their knees center stage. The lights go to black. The blue light again and this time all the INDIANS plus the YOUNG MAN and HONEY are gone. Just the DESERT TACTICAL TROOPS holding their ears and shielding their eyes. The lights stay up and become brighter. The whine and the chanting get louder, then everything goes black.

The End

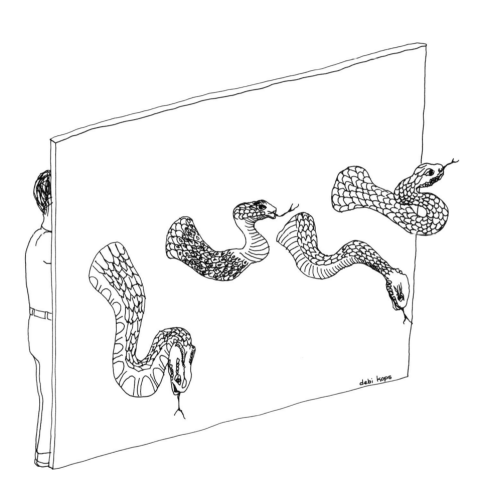

debi kops